WIGMORE ROW
CAVENDISH SQUARE
HENRIETTA STREET
CAVENDISH S.
HOLLES STR.
PRINCES STR.
CASTLE STREET
Phoenix Co.
Redlion C.
Chapel C
VERE ST.
MARYBONE LANE
O X F O
L.Holles S.
PRINCES S.
GREAT
HANOVER
Shepherd
Tenterden Street
Str.
Pedley
WOODSTOCK S.
South Moulton Row
HANOVER ST.
SQUARE
SWALLOW
NEW BOND STREET
L.BROOK S.
GREAT GEORGE STR.
MADOX STR.
Paradise R.
BackBrookS.
STREET
BROOK STREET
DAVID STREET
AVERY ROW
Brookss Mews
3 King C.
L.Madox Str.
CONDUIT STREET
GROSVENOR STREET
GROSVENOR MEWSE
BRUTON MEWSE
BRUTON STREET
Mount Row
Old Burlington M.
BURLINGTON
CLIFFORD
CORK STR.
BERKLEY
Burlington Mews
Evans Row
ALBEMARLE STREET
DOVER STREET
OLD BOND STREET
HAY HILL
BERKLEY
LES STR.

MAYFAIR

A Town Within London

From my dear wife Eva. EVA SCOTT

on my 83rd birthday. 24 July 1966.
CHARLES COWAN SCOTT
(DIED 27 SEPT, 1966)
given by Eva Scott to
Trubee Truscott Campbell
19 August 1970

Please return to
T. T. Campbell
Hillhaven Con Hosp
505 Miller Ave
Mill Valley CA 94941
415-383-8244
388-9904

Mayfair's Parish Church — St George's, Hanover Square, in 1809.
From a painting in the City of Westminster Public Library, Buckingham Palace Road.

MAYFAIR

A Town Within London

REGINALD COLBY

Foreword by the Earl of Harrowby

COUNTRY LIFE LIMITED LONDON

First published in 1966 by
Country Life Limited
Tower House, Southampton Street, London WC 2
Printed in Great Britain by
Billing & Sons Limited, Guildford and London

TO
MARGARET ILLINGWORTH
who lives in the last private house
in Grosvenor Square
WITH AFFECTION

Contents

Illustrations

HALFTONE PLATES

9

LINE BLOCKS

END PAPERS

Acknowledgments

A BOOK DESCRIBING a living part of London must depend for a great part on local lore and anecdotes handed down by those who live and work there. The spoken is just as important as the written word. I should, therefore, like to thank all those who have helped me with information. My special thanks go out to the Earl of Harrowby, whose family lived for over a century in Grosvenor Square – in the house where Lady Illingworth (to whom I am also greatly indebted) now lives; to Princess Iris Galitzine, whose grand-parents, the Duke of Cambridge and Mrs FitzGeorge, figure so largely in the chapter 'Royal Mayfair'; to Sir John Murray, who works in the same room where his ancestor John Murray II entertained Sir Walter Scott and Lord Byron; to Lady Aberconway, who opened her house in North Audley Street to me, and told me its history; to General Sir Reginald Savory, who showed me the Sussex Tankard; to Mr Hugo Houston, whose vivid memory of Mayfair reaches back to the 'nineties, when he used to attend the Mayfair Chapel; to Mr Hugh Agnew, who told me the story of 'the Stolen Duchess'; to Mr Maurice Berkeley, whose knowledge of night clubs in the 'twenties is encyclopaedic; to Mr T. M. Goode, whose firm has been established in Mayfair so long; to Mr Algernon Asprey, the director of an equally old-established Mayfair family firm; to Mr Malcolm Lyell, of Holland and Holland, who told me about the 'Bishop of Bond Street' and his dog Tiny; to Mr Harry Lawrence, the managing director of Purdey's in South Audley Street; to Mr George Brettell, whose father cut out shirts for Queen Victoria; to Mr R. Caplen, of the Grosvenor Estate; to Mr L. J. Kingston, of Gunter and Company Limited, who so kindly allowed me to browse through Gunter's old ledger; to Mr H. A. Van Thuyne of Claridge's, Mr Henry Gustave of the Connaught Hotel, Mr Fornara of the Berkeley Hotel, and Miss Julie Roberts, who helped me study the bird's-eye view of Mayfair from the topmost storey of the

Hilton Hotel. The staff of the City of Westminster Public Library in Buckingham Palace Road were particularly helpful, and I also received much assistance from the London Museum and Guildhall Libraries.

I should also like to thank the Earl of Powis, Sir Alfred Beit, Miss Rosie Newman, who used to live at 146, Piccadilly, Captain C. H. Adams, Secretary of Albany, Mr Pat Kinna and Mr Igor Vinogradoff for much useful information. Mr Harold Acton kindly read through the manuscript; Mr Tom Dowson and Mr Michael McGarvie helped with the proof reading; Mrs David Porter with the typing; Mrs Lilias Bennett gave me several most useful books on London; and Mr Aelwyn Howard-Williams, who gave valuable help with the index.

I should like also to acknowledge a great debt of gratitude to Mr Gordon Barnes, who so generously put his notes on Mayfair churches, past and present, at my disposal, without which the chapter 'Churches and Chapels' could not have been written. In this connection I should also like to thank the Rev. W. M. Atkins, Rector of St George's, the Rev. W. R. Derry, the Priest-in-Charge of the Grosvenor Chapel, and the incumbents of other Mayfair churches.

Of the books mentioned in the bibliography I should like to single out especially Mr B. H. Johnson's detailed study of the Berkeley Square neighbourhood, *Berkeley Square to Bond Street*, which has been of the greatest use.

Pending the publication of the London Survey of this section of the West End there is no detailed book on Mayfair, and this lack has emboldened me to offer my volume to the public.

Foreword

BY THE EARL OF HARROWBY

WHEN I WAS A SMALL boy at the beginning of the century my father took me to tea with Baroness Burdett-Coutts at her house in Mayfair, No. 1, Stratton Street, overlooking Green Park. She must have been about ninety years of age then, but as I look back at that afternoon so long ago it is not so much her age or the house that I remember, but rather that there was only the thinnest of thin bread-and-butter to eat for tea; no iced cakes so dear to a small boy. Doubtless I was consoled by being taken to Gunter's, only a few steps away in Berkeley Square, to eat a strawberry ice – in the days when ices were such a luxury.

This is only one of the many memories which Mr Reginald Colby's delightfully nostalgic book, *Mayfair: A Town Within London*, has called up for me.

The Baroness's house has long since been demolished, as have so many others in Mayfair. As Mr Colby points out, the despoilers have been busy there as elsewhere in London. But I am relieved to say that the house which was connected so long with my family, No. 44, Grosvenor Square, still stands, albeit somewhat precariously. When I used to visit my great-aunt there it had recently been renumbered, and I remember it having the old number 39 with two thin lines across it, either above or at the side of the new number.

My great-great-grandfather, the 1st Earl, was living there when the news of Waterloo was brought to the house on the evening of June 21st, 1815, and it was his second daughter, Mary, who in her 100th year described the scene to me – Major Percy, the Duke of Wellington's A.D.C., dashing in with the Despatch announcing the great victory. Five years later, in 1820, the house nearly became the scene of the wholesale assassination of the Cabinet by the Cato Street Conspirators.

No. 44 is still a private house, the last in Grosvenor Square. In my day nearly all the houses in Mayfair were in private hands, whereas now very few indeed are left.

St George's Church, Hanover Square, has many records of our family – christenings, weddings and such-like – as we had many homes in Mayfair. The 1st Earl's father lived successively in Hill Street and Park Street, and the 2nd Earl, before he took over the family house in Grosvenor Square at the end of 1847, had previously lived in other houses nearby. Shortly after this, in April, 1848, serious disturbances were expected from a revival of the Chartist Movement, and special constables were recruited in Mayfair to deal with possible trouble. The 2nd Earl of Harrowby was appointed Captain of the 3rd Division of the Hanover Square area, which included Bruton Street (north side), Berkeley Square (north side), Charles Street, Robert Street, Davies Street and Grosvenor Street. Among the family papers there is a large printed bill giving full particulars of the organisation of this special force, which, however, I do not think was called upon to operate. One of the eight Divisions was a single house, 23, Mount Street, Thomas Dowbiggin & Co., Cabinet Makers. Its captain was Thomas Dowbiggin. Other captains were the Duke of Leeds, the Earl of Lucan, Viscount Cantelupe, Colonel Griffith, Mr Charles Stokes and Mr Thomas Arber, surveyor and auctioneer also of Mount Street.

An ancestor of mine on the female side, the banker, John Dent, also lived in Mayfair. He was known as 'Dog Dent', being responsible for the Dog Tax which was imposed in 1808. He had property in Brick Street and lived in Hertford House in Hertford Street, dying in 1826.

Mr Colby takes us all over Mayfair, exploring its past and its present. We learn much about its churches and chapels and its great houses, we attend parties, visit the shops, mix with writers – all this not so much as spectators, but as participants. It is nothing but a privilege for me to write a foreword to this remarkable book.

CHAPTER ONE

The Fair

MAYFAIR IS A TOWN within a town – with its old market, its high street, its many churches and its world-famous hotels. Once even it had a small river and an annual fair, which gave the district its name.

Mayfair, like Soho or Bloomsbury, conjures up a part of London which for most people is difficult to define, since its boundaries are not marked on any ordnance map. Usually Mayfair is thought of as the 'ritzy' part of the West End – although the Ritz Hotel is actually not in Mayfair but in St James's.

Nevertheless Mayfair does have its boundaries, though these are unofficial. Piccadilly in its whole length from the Circus down to Hyde Park Corner separates it from St James's and Green Park on the south. Park Lane shuts it in on the western side from Hyde Park, and on the north Oxford Street divides Mayfair from Marylebone. The oblong is sealed off from Soho on the east by Regent Street, which sweeps down to Piccadilly Circus, 'hugging the West End', as Nash described his majestic thoroughfare.

This quadrilateral, in Sydney Smith's words, enclosed 'more intelligence, human ability, to say nothing of wealth and beauty than the world ever collected in so small a space before'.

Since the great spread of London to the north, west and south in the last century this concentration has been dispersed. But Mayfair still exists behind its old frontiers and, in spite of street widening, rebuilding, and one-way traffic, has largely kept its individual character of a town within a town. Nevertheless its residents are being slowly elbowed out by the western spread of offices and shops.

In the mid-nineteen-thirties there was a plan to drive an east–west highway through Mayfair from half way up Regent Street to the point where Curzon Street joins Park Lane. This would have effectively cut Mayfair in two and destroyed its compact unity. Luckily the plan was stillborn. Bond Street – Old and New – is still the only street which actually pierces Mayfair from end to end. It has existed as a thoroughfare for nearly two hundred and fifty years. As long ago as 1758 Gibbon was complaining, as he tried to study in his Bond Street lodgings, that his peace and quiet were disturbed by the noise of coaches rattling up and down the street below.

Many parts of London, now indistinguishable from the sea of houses which has engulfed them, started as villages. Knightsbridge, Chelsea, Kensington and Fulham were all villages once, but now it is difficult to say where one begins and the other ends.

Mayfair did not grow out of a village, although Shepherd Market – the heart of Mayfair – with its narrow crooked streets, small shops and old public houses, has the air of a village, and its name sounds rustic too. But a village is always built round a church, and Shepherd Market has none. The old Curzon or Mayfair Chapel in Curzon Street, demolished in 1899, dated only from 1731, and it had no predecessor. Shepherd Market has nothing to do with sheep, but derives its name from Edward Shepherd, pioneer property developer, who laid out his market on the waste ground north of Piccadilly near Hyde Park Corner. A fair, granted by King James II, used to be held on the site of the market during the first two weeks of May – the May Fair.

London then extended only as far as Air Street, near what is now Piccadilly Circus. The road to Reading led out of London to the west via Hyde Park Corner, and the land sloping down from the Oxford or Tyburn Road on its northern side – present-day Mayfair – was patterned with rolling fields and farmsteads. Many place names such as Farm Street, Hay Hill, Mill Street and Brook Street recall Mayfair's rural past; and we can still trace the undulating surface of the farmland in the contours of its streets and squares. Both Hanover Square and Berkeley Square are built on a slope, Charles Street winds up hill at the far end, probably following an old bridle path, New Bond Street dips in the centre, and if one gave a football a gentle kick at the upper end of the Burlington Arcade it would, with a little encouragement, roll down to Piccadilly, for the Arcade loses nine feet in height from one end to the other. Albany, too, is laid out on an incline. The total difference in level between Oxford Street and Piccadilly at its lowest point, the 'dip' near the St James' Club, is forty feet.

London has many underground rivers, and one of them, the Tyburn, pursues its restless course under Mayfair. It rises to the south of Hampstead, flows under Marylebone and enters Mayfair down the slope at the top end of Davies Street, and from here its course can clearly be followed. It bears immediately left by Bolding's showrooms into South Molton Lane, and then continues straight down this narrow defile as far as Brook Street, which takes its name from the old brook. Early in the 18th century the Tyburn still used to flow above ground as far as this point, as can be seen from Macky's map of St George's Parish of 1725, hanging over the staircase in the Westminster Public Library in Buckingham Palace Road, where the blue-shaded water is visible flowing down South Molton Lane.

After crossing Brook Street the Tyburn continues its straight and narrow course down Avery Row, and almost reaches New Bond Street at Lancashire Court, a quaint maze of old courts, small houses and shops. Few people turn into Lancashire Court through the narrow entrance from New Bond Street. It is one of those curious survivals in Mayfair, a colony of workshops, photographic studios, art restorers, small cafés and snack bars built on what used to be the east bank of the Tyburn. Here ducks once wandered about among the long grass and puddles, and women did their washing at the water's edge, where now two red telephone kiosks stand in the alleyway which slopes down to Avery Row, the river bed. It is said that a hospital for plague victims was built here, an isolation hospital set in the open fields.

After leaving Avery Row, the Tyburn crosses Grosvenor Street at its narrow neck near New Bond Street, flows down the steep alley of Bourdon Street and continues along the back streets (never far from New Bond Street) to Bruton Place. If we are walking down the course of the old brook – a pleasant recreation for a Saturday afternoon – we can get no further on account of a warehouse which stands right over its course and blocks our way into Bruton Street. So we have to make a detour. But after the Tyburn has crossed Bruton Street we can pick it up again in Bruton Lane at the corner of the public house in mock half-timber, the Coach and Horses, and follow the brook as it makes a wide loop round the high block of Berkeley Square House down to the bottom of Hay Hill.

Here we seem almost to be walking on the river bed itself, and can nearly believe the story that Queen Anne was rowed up the Tyburn in the royal barge as far as Brook Street, where traces of a mooring place were found during excavations there in the middle of the last century.

We can follow the Tyburn no further and must imagine it babbling along beneath our feet as we cross Berkeley Square. Sewer workers say that there is a bank of mud and shingle enclosed by a culvert just under here – all that remains of a little island formed by the Tyburn, and now the haunt of sewer rats.

The brook flows directly under old Lansdowne Passage, now shut; at one point there the paving stones are said to ring hollow where the brook passes underneath. It continues its course under Shepherd Market and falls into Piccadilly at the side of the St James' Club, where it used to flow under the 'New Bridge' into Green Park. This still causes, it is said, a mist to rise on damp nights in the autumn from the many rivulets which lose themselves in the low marshy ground on their leisurely way to the Thames. The main stream is carried in the King's Scholars Pond Sewer to Millbank.

It has been an eventful journey for the Tyburn to reach this point all the way from the hills in the north of London, and we can imagine it running down the slope between the fields before the houses were built, overflowing its banks after heavy rain.

The May Fair was held just north of Piccadilly on one of the largest fields, called Great Brookfield, bordered, as its name implies, by the Tyburn brook. It corresponded roughly to that part of Mayfair stretching on either side of Curzon Street, and covered about thirteen acres. In a good year the booths extended into the surrounding fields.

The fair was not held here until the reign of King James II, and should not be confused with the St James's Fair which took place near the site of present day St James's Square in July and had mediaeval origins. Letters patent were granted in 1686 and 1688 to hold a market for live cattle on May 1st every year for fourteen days on Brookfield near Hyde Park Corner which was then a rural cross-roads. A cluster of simple taverns stood at this gateway to London, frequented by drovers who brought their cattle to town.

The cattle fair soon became an excuse for a general jollification, and the citizens feeling in need of a breath of fresh country air after being pent up in the close built city all winter streamed out of London to celebrate the coming of spring. A host of hucksters and entertainers surged out with them, and early in the cattle fair's existence Great Brookfield and the neighbouring fields presented a gay and lively scene with tents and booths spread over the fresh green grass and the spring air vibrating with excitement as the multitudes of Londoners flocked to amuse themselves on the roundabouts and swings, tried their luck at the gambling tables, sampled the sausage stalls, gazed open-mouthed at the mountebanks, jugglers and Indian rope dancers, and were made to laugh and cry in turn by the antics of the tinsel heroes on the antique stages.

The fair grew in size and scope as each May came round, and sometimes a topical note was added as in May, 1696, when an impresario named Miller put on a show glorifying King William III's resounding success over the French at the Siege of Namur.

WILLIAM REX
May Fair
Miller's
or the Loyal Association Booth
at the upper end of
Brook-field Market
near Hyde Park Corner
During the time of May-Fair will be presented
an excellent droll called
KING WILLIAM'S HAPPY DELIVERANCE
and glorious triumph over his enemies
or The Consultation of the
POPE, DEVIL, FRENCH KING and the GRAND TURK.
With the whole Form of the Siege of NAMUR
And the humours of a Renegade French Man
and BRANDY JEAN
With the conceits of Scaramouch and Harlequin
Together with the best singing and Dancing that
was ever seen in a Fair, also a Dialogue Song
VIVAT REX

Inevitably as the May Fair grew in size and popularity it became a resort for the riff-raff of the town and earned a bad reputation for itself. The merry-making went on all night, and when Queen Anne came to the throne and a wave of puritanism swept the country, its existence was threatened. The Queen thoroughly disapproved of such a disorderly crowd meeting within half a mile of St James's Palace at the far end of Piccadilly, as the noise of their revelling would have been clearly audible for miles around in the London of those days, when sound travelled so much more freely.

In 1702 the authorities took action to prevent undesirables from entering the fair ground, and provoked a near riot, for the constables apprehended three girls as prostitutes by mistake, and in the fighting that followed a constable named John Cooper was run through with a rapier and killed. Later, one Thomas Cook, a butcher and prize fighter, was arrested in Ireland, found guilty of murder and hanged at Tyburn. The Justices of the Peace decided to draw attention to the disorderly fair, and so bring it into discredit, by giving the constable a public funeral at St James's, Piccadilly, and afterwards they ordered a sermon to be published with its carefully chosen text:

> Then stood up Phineas and executed Judgement and so the plague was stayed. (Psalm 106, v. 30)

But the fair was not stayed yet. A few years had to pass before an end was put to the annual explosion of high spirits on Brookfield. Then in 1708 the Grand Jury of Westminster, encouraged by the example of the magistrates of the City of London in their proceedings against the Bartholomew Fair,

> presented as a publick nuisance and inconvenience the yearly riotous and tumultuous assembly, in a place called Brookfield in the Parish of St Martin-in-the-Fields in this county, called May-Fair in which place many loose, idle and disorderly persons do rendez-vous and draw and allure young persons and servants to meet to game and commit lewd and disorderly practices . . .

Several other presentments followed and finally a Royal Proclamation strictly enjoined the proprietors and owners of the Fair

> not to permit any booths or stalls to be erected while the Fair should be holden for any plays, shews, gaming, music, meetings or other disorderly assemblies.

This meant the end of the May Fair – as long as Queen Anne lived, and in April, 1709, the *Tatler* advised any of its readers who might be thinking of enjoying the fun of the fair that it was 'utterly abolished' and that Mr Penkethman, a well-known entertainer and the owner of a menagerie, who travelled round the country, 'had removed his ingenious company of strollers to Greenwich'. The paper added mischievously that should any lady or gentleman have occasion to buy a tame elephant 'let them enquire of Mr Penkethman who had one to dispose of at a reasonable price'; also that a tiger would sell almost as cheap as an ox, and a cat with three legs could be purchased 'for very near the value of one with four'.

Not content with their action, the authorities published their *Reasons for suppressing the yearly Fair in Brookfield Westminster, commonly called May Fair*. In thundering language the terrible indictment stated that it

> had been of ill consequence, tending to corrupt the minds and manners of many people inasmuch that it is now one of the most pestilent nurseries of impurity and vice,

that the multitude of its booths were not for trade and merchandise, but for

> musick, showes, drinking, gaming, raffling, lotteries, stage plays and drolls which are constant and open scenes of impiety and profaneness and very frequently the stalls of vice and impurities not to be mentioned.

Gone were the gay days of the Restoration. This was almost a return to the stern era of Cromwell. However, the wave of High Church feeling sweeping over the country which suppressed the May Fair (although it only lasted a mere fourteen days) also gave us some of London's finest eighteenth-century churches, among them St George's, Hanover Square, Mayfair's parish church.

The May Fair could be suppressed but not abolished. The Royal Proclamation did not prohibit the Fair from being held. For such a step an Act of Parliament would have been necessary, as the grants from James II to hold a fair 'in the field called Brook-field' included the words 'for ever'. The grants had been abused, hence the Royal Proclamation, but when Queen Anne died and there was a relaxation of High Church tension the auspices for reviving the May Fair seemed more favourable. Her Hanoverian successors, the first two Georges, both born in the land of fairs, had a 'continental' attitude towards public entertainment. If they did not encourage the Fair, they certainly did not discourage it, and gradually the amusements, side shows, jugglers, drolls, Tiddy-Dol – the celebrated seller of gingerbread who figures in Hogarth's well-known picture of the *Apprentice's Execution at Tyburn* – all returned to their former haunts.

The old fairs had begun to die in London – not so much because of outraged morals, but for lack of space. Those of Drury Lane and St James's were no more. The celebrated Maypole in the Strand had been taken down in April, 1718. St Bartholomew's Fair was not what it was. The fast growing metropolis was driving out of existence these picturesque survivals of the Middle Ages. The revived May Fair was almost the last in London, and became all the more popular for this reason. But it had dwindled in size for there had been enormous building activity since its suppression, and the open fields were nearly all covered with streets and squares.

Edward Shepherd had already started his building operations on Brookfield, leasing his land from the ground landlord, Sir Nathaniel Curzon, and it was in a greatly restricted area centring on his new market that the booths, stalls and sideshows were set up. However, there was still room on the neighbouring waste land for the Fair's great attraction – duck hunting.

This barbarous sport – practised by the market butchers – needed a pond large enough to give the duck plenty of space in which to try to escape from the pursuing dogs. The Master of the Hunt put the duck in the water with its wings pinioned and the dogs were then let loose after it. The duck would dive as often as possible, until at last more dead than alive it would be seized by one of the dogs – spaniels excelled at this 'sport' – which brought it back to land and laid it at the feet of its master to the great applause of the crowd who stood around the pond under the trees, and were only prevented from falling into the water in their excitement by a low wooden fence around the edge.

Duck hunting left many traces behind in Mayfair as evidence of its popularity. There used to be an old half-timbered public house with a garden attached at the lower end of Hertford Street called the Dog and Duck. Ducking Pond Mews was near here, and Ducking Pond Row was the original name of Grafton Street, the short cut to the fair-ground from Old Bond Street.

The Three Jolly Butchers, kept by Francis Beachum, was another public house in this old part of Mayfair. During the Fair a stage was erected in front of it, and it was here that Henry Woodward made his début as Merry Andrew in a theatrical career which eventually took him to Drury Lane. The shops and market stalls were converted into booths, and a grocer with the Italian sounding name of Fritti let out part of his premises for a puppet show where mock executions were held. A puppet laid its head on the block and it was immediately chopped off by another puppet – to great applause, as Mayfair was loyal to the Hanoverians, and everyone knew that the execution represented the beheading of Jacobite Lord Lovat for high treason.

Soon the name May Fair, written in two distinct words, was given to the district of narrow streets, alleyways, public houses, coffee houses, and little shops which grew up around Edward Shepherd's market. Francis Beachum, the landlord of the Three Jolly Butchers, Thomas Bronley who kept the coffee house, William Bennet the butcher, and James Bucher the potter, all gave their address as May Fair when they voted in the Westminster bye-election of 1749.

For over a century afterwards Mayfair was still spelt – and pronounced – in two words. Thackeray still uses the name May Fair to describe this fashionable part of London in his novel *Vanity Fair* which he wrote in 1849. By then the old fair had been closed down for more than eighty years, but in his youth old inhabitants could still remember it or had heard about it from their fathers.

John Carter, who was born near Carter's stonemason's yard in Piccadilly, wrote down his reminiscences for the *Gentleman's Magazine* in March, 1816:

> Fifty years have passed since this place of amusement was at its height of attraction. The spot where the fair was held still retains the name of May Fair, and exists in much the same state as at the above period . . . The Market House consists of two stories, first storey a long and cross aisle for butchers' shops, externally other shops connected with culinary purposes. Second storey used as a theatre at fair time for dramatic performances.

He tells us that the butchers had to vacate their stalls during the fortnight of the fair and their places were taken by 'Toy-men and gingerbread-makers'.

The May Fair did not achieve its centenary. No Act of Parliament suppressed it. The thrust of the town westwards was already threatening to stifle it out of existence when the new residents at the western end of Piccadilly began to object to the outburst of noise occurring every first of May. Up till then this stretch of Piccadilly opposite Green Park had been lined with popular taverns like the Half Moon, the Greyhound Inn and the White Horse, and a row of untidy looking stonemason's yards with narrow alleys leading deviously between them into the fair-ground.

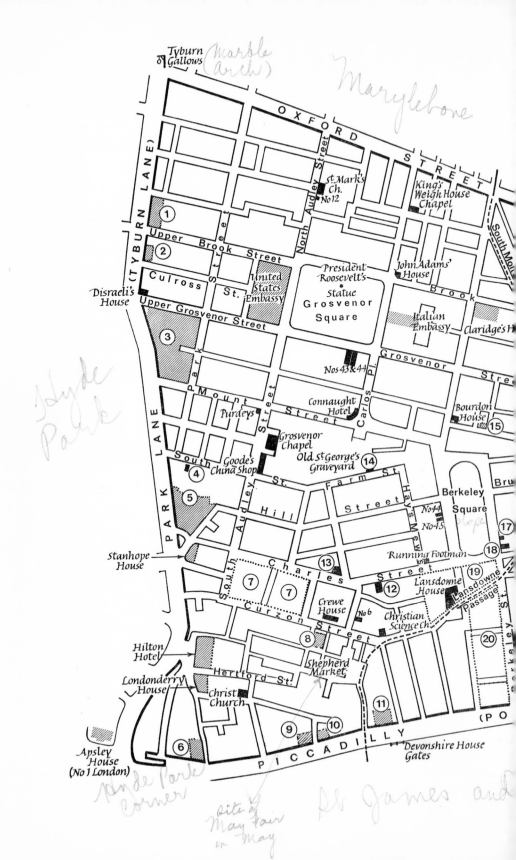

Tyburn Gallows

Marble (Arch)

Marylebone

OXFORD STREET

TYBURN LANE (TYBURN LANE)

1

Upper Brook Street

2

St. Mark's Ch. No 12

North Audley Street

King's Weigh House Chapel

South Mol

Culross

Disraeli's House

United States Embassy

St.

John Adams' House

President Roosevelt's

Statue

Grosvenor Square

Brook

Claridge's H

Italian Embassy

Upper Grosvenor Street

3

Park

Nos 43 & 44

Grosvenor

Str

Carlos Pl.

Mount Street

Purdeys

Connaught Hotel

Bourdon House

15

PARK LANE

Grosvenor Chapel

Street

Old St. George's Graveyard

14

South

Goode's China Shop

4

Audley

St.

Farm St.

Street

Hays Mews

Berkeley Square

Bru

Hill

Street

No 44

No 45

ope

17

5

18

Stanhope House

Charles

13

Running Footman

19

South

7

7

12

Lansdowne House

Lansdowne

Passage

Crewe House

No 6

Christian Science Ch.

Curzon

8

Street

20

Hilton Hotel

Londonderry House

Hertford St.

Shepherd Market

Berkeley St.

Christ Church

11

(P O

9

10

Apsley House (No 1 London)

6

Devonshire House Gates

PICCADILLY

Hyde Park Corner

site of May Fair in May

St James and

Hyde Park

MAP OF MAYFAIR
PAST AND PRESENT

1. Brook House
2. Dudley House
3. Grosvenor House, now Grosvenor House (Hotel)
4. Site of Florence Nightingale's house
5. Dorchester House, now Dorchester Hotel
6. Site of 2nd Duke of Cambridge's house
7. Site of Chesterfield House and garden
8. Sunderland House on site of the Mayfair Chapel
9. Lord Coventry's House, now St James' Club
10. Site of Pulteney Hotel
11. Cambridge House, now Naval and Military Club
12. 37, Charles Street, the English-Speaking Union
13. Site of Berkeley Chapel
14. Farm Street Church
15. Site of St Mary's Church
16. Site of Queen Elizabeth II's birth place
17. Site of No 11, Horace Walpole's house
18. Site of Gunter's
19. Site of Lansdowne House garden
20. Site of Devonshire House and garden
21. Site of Clarendon (later Albemarle) House
22. Site of Trinity Chapel, now Westbury Hotel
23. Site of Hanover Chapel
24. Site of Harewood House

Course of Tyburn - - - - -

Soon fine buildings began to take their place and when the old Grey-hound Inn was pulled down and Sir Henry Hunloke built himself a grand house on the site, later bought by the Earl of Coventry, the fate of the May Fair was sealed. Lord Coventry's house (now the St James' Club) backed on the fair-ground and he made a complaint to the Parish about the noise. As in good Queen Anne's day the proprietors of the booths and stalls were enjoined not to allow their premises to be used for disorderly purposes. This was the end, and the May Fair was silenced for ever (though an attempt was made to revive it in the 1950s) leaving only its name behind now joined as one word – Mayfair.

CHAPTER TWO

Piccadilly Frontier

THE PAIR OF MAGNIFICENT blue and gold armorial gates standing in Piccadilly on the edge of Green Park lead nowhere and are kept permanently locked. Once they had railings on either side of them in the days when Green Park – and Hyde Park, too – were railed in, but they were torn down for scrap in the last war and the gates now stand there looking extremely elegant, though serving no purpose.

The gates have swung open and shut in their time in front of three great mansions. They first adorned Lord Heathfield's house at Turnham Green, and when this house was demolished the Duke of Devonshire bought them and set them up in front of his Palladian villa at Chiswick, built by his ancestor, the Earl of Burlington, and when Chiswick House was sold, they were placed in front of Devonshire House in Piccadilly, which until then had been hidden from the street by a high brick wall, with plain heavy wooden gates at either end.

Londoners disliked this long brown brick wall skirting Piccadilly. Grim and ugly it gave the impression of hostile and barricaded seclusion as if the noble owner wanted to have nothing to do with the common world outside – which was in fact the reason for it being there in the first place, as it dated from the time when nearly every great London house used to be shut off from the street by a high wall. As long ago as 1783 it had annoyed Londoners and was referred to as 'this execrable brick screen'.

By the eighteen-nineties the Devonshire House wall became so unpopular that a press campaign was started to have it removed. Max Beerbohm added his not so gentle voice to the clamour, but he wished the wall to be left where it was and castigated those who wanted to infringe the privacy of the great house by pulling it down and opening up the courtyard to the public gaze. The Duke of Devonshire compromised. He retained the wall, but lightened its severity by putting the gates from Chiswick in the centre, forming an elegant approach to his house from Piccadilly, as we can see from Howard Penton's drawing.

The old brick wall had its uses, however. It screened the house from prying eyes so effectively that when bicycling became the craze for ladies in the 'nineties, friends of Louise, Duchess of Devonshire, used to practise riding their uncertain machines in the spacious courtyard of Devonshire House and could wobble about to their heart's content without being spied at from the street, though their shrieks may well have puzzled passers-by in Piccadilly.

The old wall was a historical relic, having originally screened Berkeley House, built for Lord Berkeley of Stratton in 1666 by Hugh May. A rough track, hardly improved since the Middle Ages and infested by footpads, climbed up the hill from Hyde Park Corner to Lord Berkeley's house, which was the first building of any consequence the traveller passed as his coach lumbered into town, the 'No 1, London' of those days; the 'mountainous villages' of Hampstead and Highgate could be seen over the garden at the back.

A little further along Portugal Street, as this stretch of Piccadilly was then called after King Charles II's Portuguese wife, stood Clarendon House, an even more magnificent house on the same side of the street fronted with a courtyard and also backed by a large formal garden running into the fields. Then the traveller passed by Burlington House, built by Richard Boyle, first Earl of Burlington, originally of red brick before his great-grandson, the architect earl, rebuilt it so elegantly some fifty years later.

These three grand houses stood in line on a large plot of land granted by the Crown to Lord Clarendon, the Lord Chancellor, who kept the best site for himself in the centre opposite St James's Palace and sold off the plots on either side.

Property development in this area started surprisingly early. Clarendon House, the first of the mansions to be built, was the first to vanish. A handsome, well-proportioned building, it was designed by Sir Roger Pratt in 1664, and its rows of large sash windows – an expensive luxury three hundred years ago – looked down the hill at the old palace which seemed modest and homely in comparison with the new house the Lord Chancellor had built himself.

If we stand in the trough of St James's in front of the old red brick palace and look up the hill, we can see what an excellent site Lord Clarendon chose for his house, which covered the plot of land between present day Dover Street and Old Bond Street, reaching as far back as Grafton Street. John Evelyn, a friend of Sir Roger Pratt, whom he had known in Rome, 'projected' the garden at the back. He greatly admired Clarendon House.

Samuel Pepys, too, was enraptured by Clarendon House and, always eager to see the latest marvel, he climbed up to the roof before the house was even finished and called the view 'the noblest prospect I ever saw in my life'.

Hardly had Clarendon moved into his new palace when he fell from power and was forced to flee the country. Shortly afterwards the second Duke of Albemarle, General Monck's son, bought the Lord Chancellor's house and renamed it Albemarle House, only to sell it in his turn to a syndicate headed by John Hinde, a goldsmith-banker, who pulled the fine house down and developed the site – within twenty years after its erection. Thus early in Mayfair's history the pattern was set for the destruction of its great houses.

Mayfair's first streets were laid out on the site: Dover Street, Albemarle Street and Bond Street, with the short Stafford Street traversing them. It is remarkable to think that in nearly three hundred years they have not changed their names (except that Bond Street soon became Old Bond Street when it was extended into New Bond Street) or their width or length. But their character has been completely transformed.

These four streets were planned as the nucleus of a new part of town above St James's on the edge of open country, intended to draw the nobility and gentry from their traditional places of residence in Covent Garden and the City, left in ruins after the Great Fire.

Bond Street took its name from Sir Thomas Bond, a member of John Hinde's syndicate, who had been Comptroller of Queen Henrietta Maria's household in France, where he married a French woman. He was created a baronet for services, mainly financial, rendered to King Charles II. Others who took up leases on Albemarle Ground – as the site of Albemarle House was called – were Henry Jermyn, later Lord Dover, and Margaret Stafford, both of whose names, like Sir Thomas Bond's, live on in these, the earliest streets of Mayfair.

Bond Street (today Old Bond Street) was named in 1686, the year after Bond died. It ran into open country at the northern end where now New Bond Street begins. John Macky writes in his *Journey through*

England of 1714 that 'the Earl Paulet, late Lord Steward of the House-hold, lived in a most magnificent palace' in Bond Street, with a fine prospect of the adjacent country. Macky's use of the word palace for the new house is significant. 'All Bond Street is palaces', he wrote; so carried away was this Scotsman with the magnificence of London's new residential quarter that he forgot his grammar.

Stafford Street was completed in the same year as Bond Street, as we can see from Mayfair's oldest relic, the Stafford Street sign, in the Duke of Albemarle public house at the corner of Stafford Street and Dover Street. It is fixed to the wall on the right of the door and the carved inscription can be read quite distinctly:

This is Stafford S$^{ET}_{TR}$ 1686

Hinde's syndicate also planned to lay out a square of three acres on Albemarle Ground to be called Albemarle Square at the top of Dover Street, Albemarle Street and Bond Street, but nothing came of it as the syndicate went bankrupt.

Building fever also spread further down Piccadilly and speculators fixed their eyes on Berkeley House. Its owner, Lord Berkeley, Lord Lieutenant of Ireland, died in 1678 and his widow, Lady Berkeley, felt tempted, if not to sell the house, at least to let out some of its grounds in building leases.

Before making any decision, however, she called in the old family friend, John Evelyn, for advice. He had seen the house being built and admired its many noble rooms, its cedar staircase, its princely furniture and above all its 'incomparable gardens' and the 'pretty piscina'. Lady Berkeley planned to cut strips off her garden at either side. Evelyn could not but deplore her decision and noted regretfully in his diary on June 12th, 1684:

> I went to advise and give direction about the building two streetes in Berkeley Gardens reserving the house and as much of the garden as the breadth of the house. In the meantime I could not but deplore that sweete place should be so much straiten'd and turned into tene-ments. But that magnificent pile and gardens contiguous to it, built by the late Lord Chancellor Clarendon, being all demolish'd, and designed for piazzas and buildings, was some excuse for my Lady Berkeley's resolution of letting out her ground also for so excessive a price as was offered advancing neere £1000 per ann. in mere

ground-rents; to such a mad intemperance was the age come of building about a Citty, by far too disproportionate already to the nation: I having in my time seene it almost as large again as it was within my memory.

The two new streets carved out of the garden of Berkeley House were named Stratton Street and Berkeley Street, first mentioned in the rate books in 1693 and 1698 respectively, commemorating the family name and title of the ground landlord. They were to prove extremely profitable to the Berkeley family for over two hundred years, thanks to Lady Berkeley's keen business sense (she was the daughter of Sir Andrew Riccard, a London merchant and Chairman of the East India Company). Today these streets flank the block of Devonshire House and the distance between them corresponds to the length of the much-hated wall. While the 'tenements' – to use Evelyn's quaint expression – were being built, Lady Berkeley, combining her business acumen with a strong social sense, found an extremely suitable tenant for the family house – none other than the heir presumptive to the throne.

Princess Anne, who was on bad terms with her sister, Queen Mary, over her bosom friend Sarah Churchill, needed a house, and Berkeley House suited her requirements admirably, being large, up to date, in the fashionable new district and not too far from St James's Palace, which had taken the place of Whitehall as the royal residence. The Princess found her landlord a tough customer to deal with, however, and wrote to Sarah:

> I was yesterday at Berkeley House, which I like very well, but my Lady looked so mightily out of humour that I did not go into all the garrets nor the wings as I intended, and until she goes out of the house it will be impossible to order anything or see it at one's ease; and when she be pleased to remove God knows.

Eventually in 1692 Princess Anne and her husband, Prince George of Denmark, moved in, taking Berkeley House at £600 a year for three years – the first royal residents of Mayfair.

Her arrival was celebrated by the Bellman of Piccadilly who wrote these charming verses to the Princess Anne of Denmark:

> *Welcome, great princess to this lowly place*
> *Where injured royalty must hide its face;*
> *Your praise each day by every man is sung*
> *And in the night shall here by me be rung.*

31

God bless our Queen! And yet may I moreover
Own you our Queen in Berkeley Street and Dover;
May you and your great prince live numerous years!
This is the subject of our loyal prayers.

She did not bring her little five-year-old son, William, Duke of Gloucester with her as the country air of Kensington was thought to be better for his fragile health. On her birthday in February, however, he came to see her at Berkeley House accompanied by a guard of honour composed of about a dozen boys a few years older than himself, the miniature officers wearing feathers in their caps and the soldiers red helmets.

On Queen Mary's death in 1694 the situation completely changed. Princess Anne became a personage in her own right and instead of being cold shouldered by the court she found herself surrounded by courtiers and time servers who came to Berkeley House – now bathed with a special radiance – to bow before the rising sun of monarchy. King William, too, visited her as a token of their improved relations after his wife's death and finally offered her St James's Palace as a residence while he lived on alone at Kensington Palace.

During her residence at Berkeley House Princess Anne probably took her lasting dislike of the May Fair, as her back windows almost overlooked the fairground, and crowds went streaming past the house all day and night during the rollicking fortnight of merrymaking.

Just before she left Berkeley House an event occurred which was a sign of things to come. No. 94 of *The Postman* for 1695 published an advertisement that a silver cistern valued at £250 had been stolen from Berkeley House, the property of its royal tenants. The cistern was eventually found in the possession of a distiller in Twickenham, who was caught and convicted, the first of a long succession of highwaymen, footpads, pickpockets, dog stealers, purse snatchers, cat burglars and their modern successors, jewel and fur thieves, who have found Mayfair such a profitable sphere of operations.

Princess Anne's residence at Berkeley House, short though it was, had repercussions, for as usually happens when royalty sets its seal of approval there was a rush to follow her there.

Two of the most prominent men of the day, William Cavendish, recently created Duke of Devonshire, and John Sheffield, Marquess of Normanby, later Duke of Buckingham, both wanted to buy Berkeley

1. A MAY FAIR IN 1716. The fair held every May in the fields north of Piccadilly on the site of Shepherd Market gave its name to present-day Mayfair. (Radio Times, Hulton Picture Library)

2. BERKELEY HOUSE. Old Berkeley House, built in 1665 by Lord Berkeley of Stratton, stood in open country where Berkeley Street meets Piccadilly. Bought by the first Duke of Devonshire, it was rebuilt by William Kent as Devonshire House. (Crace Collection, British Museum)

3. DEVONSHIRE HOUSE. Devonshire House stood back from Piccadilly sheltered by its high wall. The armorial gates — from Chiswick House — now grace Green Park. Drawn by Howard Penton.

4. THE DESTRUCTION OF DEVONSHIRE HOUSE. The famous Piccadilly landmark was demolished in 1924. Etching by Job Nixon by permission of Mrs J. Nixon.

House. The third Lord Berkeley, Lady Berkeley's second son, who lacked his mother's good sense, was in charge of negotiations. Each made an offer, and he 'sold' it to both. There were such complications over the double 'sale' that the Duke of Devonshire brought the matter to the Court of Chancery. He finally won the case – Lord Berkeley died before it was over – and he was rated in respect of Berkeley House in 1697, paying £11,000 for it. An important clause was included in the sale: Lord Berkeley and his heirs agreed not to build on their land to the north of Berkeley House within the breadth of the garden which 'might annoy' the house – a vital factor governing the formation, or rather non-formation of Berkeley Square. Soon after the Duke of Devonshire took up residence in his new house, King William honoured him with his presence at dinner there, and in the new reign he was Lord High Steward at the coronation of Queen Anne. So began the long and illustrious association of the noble house of Cavendish with Mayfair.

Lord Normanby, having lost his right to Berkeley House, bought Arlington House at the western end of the Mall instead, and after he was created Duke of Buckingham he set about rebuilding it, renaming his new home Buckingham House. Had he, instead of the Duke of Devonshire, moved into Berkeley House he would have had no need to build himself a new house and there would have been no Buckingham Palace today.

Burlington House, the third of the great houses on the Piccadilly fringe of Mayfair, has survived, but not in its original form. The present palatial Burlington House, home of the Royal Academy and many other learned societies, with Pennethorne's rich and festive show-piece at the back in Burlington Gardens (opened by Queen Victoria in the pouring rain on May 11th, 1870) is the result of many waves of rebuilding.

The first Earl of Burlington built here because he was determined to live facing the open country, and as we can see from the Jan Kip engraving of 1707 he enjoyed the same uninterrupted view to the north as his neighbours, Lords Clarendon and Berkeley. To the east the narrower strip of formal garden belonged to the fourth house on the north side of Portugal Street, built by Sir Thomas Clarges. Next to nothing is known about his house – it is a mystery building of which the only picture is the fragment in the right hand corner of the engraving. But we can see the garden in its full length stretching into the fields. Sir William Chambers rebuilt the house in 1771 for George Lamb, the first Viscount Melbourne, and the 'Mansion' facing Piccadilly became the nucleus of the unique Mayfair institution which has come down almost untouched

C   33

since Regency days: Albany. It takes its name from the second title of the Duke of York and Albany who lived here for a few years until 1802 when the 'Mansion' was converted into sets of chambers for bachelors, and two new ranges were laid out on the garden with the 'Rope Walk' leading between them to Albany's back entrance in Burlington Gardens.

The third Earl of Burlington, the 'architect Earl' and creator of Chiswick House, remodelled his grandfather's house in Piccadilly soon after he came of age in 1715. He worked closely with his architects, especially after his first visit to Italy, and Londoners were amazed to see an Italian *palazzo* take the place of the old Carolean red brick house. It was largely the work of James Gibbs, who also built the semi-circular colonnade inside the courtyard, thought once to have been designed by the Earl himself.

The Earl of Burlington landed himself so deeply in debt owing to his passion for the arts – he was the patron of writers, artists and architects – that he had to develop his estate to the north of the house, Ten Acre Close, to raise money. But London was the gainer. Each house he built, and many of them he designed himself, was a little masterpiece. Although only a few of his houses remain, the Cork Street–Savile Row area of Mayfair still preserves the intimate character he gave it. The streets are mostly short and narrow and end in a cross street where he planned the vista to be filled by some architectural feature. Cork Street was lined with trees which added to its secluded air, and leafy branches hung down over the high wall at the back of Burlington House in Vigo Lane, today Burlington Gardens.

One house more than all the others aroused the admiration of Lord Burlington's contemporaries – the Palladian *palazzino* he built for General Wade in Old Burlington Street. Lord Chesterfield said of it that to be sure he could not live in it, but he would take the house opposite and enjoy looking at it. Later it became the Burlington Hotel, and Florence Nightingale used to stay there, making it her 'Little War Office' when she was at the height of her fame after the Crimean War. Needless to say it was destroyed in the nineteen-thirties.

At the end of the 18th century this quiet corner of Mayfair changed in character. The aristocratic residents moved out, and the doctors moved in. Nearly every house became the home of an eminent physician. Sir William Farquhar, William Pitt's doctor, lived at 36, Conduit Street; Dr Eliotson, who saved Thackeray's life as we are reminded in the introduction to *Pendennis*, lived at No. 37, and Sir Astley Cooper, who had the most fashionable practice in London, at No. 39. Savile Row, too, became a street of physicians like Harley Street today. Wheatley writing in 1870 says that this once fashionable street was 'now almost entirely inhabited by eminent physicians and surgeons, who occupy nearly every house in the street'. They lived in style and it was customary for a fashionable doctor to drive to see his patients in an elegant carriage and pair with a 'tiger' sitting beside the coachman on the box, his arms crossed and elbows out as tradition prescribed.

Lady Holland, 'Old Madagascar', the hostess of Holland House in Kensington, had her winter quarters here, living in Cork Street. Remembering her constant preoccupation with her health, she must have been in her element with every eminent doctor in London on her doorstep.

Later on there was another change of population in this neighbourhood, and consulting rooms were turned into cutting and fitting rooms as the doctors moved out and the tailors took over the old Georgian houses. Many of them are there still, though demolition is beginning to make this part of Mayfair unrecognisable. Almost one whole side of Savile Row has been rebuilt, and it was a sad day when the splendid premises of Henry Poole and Co, the well-known tailors founded in 1828, were pulled down and that Savile Row landmark – a huge crown resting on a tasselled scarlet cushion – vanished from view. Henry Poole, who made suits for the Prince of Wales and the Emperor Napoleon III, had great social gifts, and Disraeli is said to have taken him as his model for 'Mr Vigo' of Burlington Street, the fashionable tailor in *Endymion* who drove the finest horses in London, and whose villa on the Thames, 'The Cedars', once belonged to a noble customer.

Disraeli in his old age went to a tailor named Jackson in Cork Street, but his clothes never fitted him as his wife impressed on the tailor when he called to take his measurements not to pay any attention to her husband's stoop but to make the coat for a young man who stood upright. She also chose the materials and colours.

Building fever caught on all over Mayfair in the first years of the 18th century, and every day streets pushed their way further into the open land that still stretched between present day Regent Street and the fair-ground. It is a pity that no artist sketched the scene of the half constructed streets ending abruptly in waste land, the houses enclosed in their wooden scaffolding and plumes of smoke rising up on all sides from the innumerable brick kilns on the building sites. Residents who had already moved into their new houses complained strongly about the stench and the noise and many brought law suits against the builders or owners of the land, claiming damages.

Rents went up and up and soon Lady Berkeley's £1000, which had so impressed Evelyn, began to seem quite small. The City Fathers found that they had made a bad deal when they leased out Conduit Mead to Lord Clarendon in 1666 at a ground rent of £6 a year for 99 years. It was reckoned that leases in Mayfair which were originally negotiated to bring in a niggardly £2 a year were worth £1776 a year by 1743 – so steep was the rise in property values in the West End. It has not stopped rising since, and in 1964 the freehold of the block at the corner of Dover Street and Piccadilly was sold for £797,000.

The following lines of doggerel by James Bramston in *The Art of Politicks*, published in 1729, show how a contemporary poet viewed the rapid changes occurring before his eyes in this part of London:

> *What's not destroyed by Time's devouring hand?*
> *Where's Troy, and where's the Maypole in the Strand?*
> *Peases, cabbages and turnips grew, where*
> *Now stands New Bond Street and a newer square,*
> *Such piles of buildings now rise up and down,*
> *London itself seems growing out of town.*

Sir Robert Walpole, while he was Prime Minister, did not visit this part of town – since it was contrary to etiquette for a Prime Minister in office to return visits, but once out of office in 1742 he took the opportunity of visiting a few of his friends, and happening to pass Berkeley Square found an entirely new part of London that he had never seen before.

Since his last visit a new Berkeley House, or Devonshire House as it was now called, had been built. In 1733 a disastrous fire, caused by a workman upsetting a pot of glue over some shavings, entirely destroyed Hugh May's house which had stood at the gateway to London for over 60 years. In its place the 4th Duke of Devonshire employed William Kent to build him a new house, the rather plain but well-proportioned building which we see in Howard Penton's drawing, compared by some to a barracks or a workhouse. The notorious wall which so annoyed Londoners at the end of the last century was all that survived of the original Berkeley House after the fire.

Plain and simple from the outside, Devonshire House was sumptuous within. The 6th Duke of Devonshire, who had a passion for improving his property, carried out large scale alterations in 1840, redecorating the state rooms in a lavish style and adding the famous gently ascending staircase with its gilded ironwork and glass handrail of which it was said that 'going up it was like coming down another'. One room he left untouched – his mother's boudoir hung in blue and silver. His mother was the beautiful Duchess Georgiana, Queen of London Society, whose debts almost equalled those of the royal Dukes and whose kisses played such an important part in winning the Westminster Election of 1784 for her friend Charles James Fox and the Whig cause.

Devonshire House with its high brick wall remained a Piccadilly landmark until shortly after the first World War when the Duke of Devonshire sold it, but it was not demolished immediately owing to the postwar slump and it served many purposes while the future of this extremely valuable site of 161,000 square feet in the heart of the West End was decided. One would-be buyer wanted to turn it into a cinema and amusement centre. It was often used for charity purposes and the last function held there was a costume ball in December, 1924, and hardly had the guests walked down the famous staircase in their 18th-century costumes when workmen started pulling the historic old house apart.

Long before Devonshire House was demolished rumours had circulated that the house was to be sold, and Louise Duchess of Devonshire grew so tired of hearing the same old story that one day she told a particularly inquisitive questioner in her strong German accent that she and the Duke had taken a house on Clapham Common: 'There is such a very good train service to London from there, you know!'

The Duchess, born Louise von Alten, was known as the 'Double Duchess' because she married two dukes, first the Duke of Manchester, and after his death the Duke of Devonshire. She was one of the great hostesses of her day, and her reign at Devonshire House and at Chatsworth, – where she entertained King Edward VII – recalled the brilliant days of Duchess Georgiana.

Devonshire House was the first of the great houses of Mayfair to be pulled down in this century, and marked the beginning of a chapter which has still not ended. The destruction of such a famous landmark caused a sensation even in those Philistine days, and the sight of a historic 18th-century house being pulled down by a gang of 20th-century English workmen was sufficiently novel for artists to come and draw the scene. When the dust had settled in both senses of the word an unsightly gap was revealed in Piccadilly to remind Londoners of the crime that had been committed. A month or two earlier all the fine trees of Devonshire House garden had been felled, and in December, 1925, a widened Berkeley Street was opened replacing the shady lane which used to lead to Berkeley Square from Piccadilly, while the steel framework of the present twelve-storey Devonshire House grew higher and higher.

The old house in Piccadilly has not vanished without trace. The armorial gates, which used to lead into the courtyard, stand in splendid isolation on the edge of Green Park bearing the punning motto of the House of Cavendish *Cavendo Tutus* – Secure by Caution – and the stone urns and lodges crossed the Atlantic to be re-erected at Glencoe on Long Island.

Now as one looks at this busy corner of Piccadilly with one-way traffic pouring out of Berkeley Square it is difficult to believe that a private house once stood here with its wooded garden stretching down Berkeley Street.

CHAPTER THREE

Mayfair Squares

BERKELEY SQUARE grew slowly owing to difficulties over leases and building contracts and also to the lack of drive shown by Lady Berkeley's sons. The restrictive covenant imposed on Lord Berkeley and his heirs restraining them from building on the south side so as not 'to annoy' Devonshire House prevented Berkeley Square from being completed until shortly before the last war when the present large block was built on the site of Lansdowne House garden, there being by then no Devonshire House to 'annoy'.

As Max Beerbohm says, Berkeley Square 'has no squareness': the east and west sides are much longer than the south and north, and it is also laid out on a slope which adds to its individuality among London squares. One can imagine a wood or pasture land running down to the lush banks of the Tyburn which meandered acrosss the eastern corner of the square before the houses came.

The east side was built first and was named Berkeley Row, being a continuation of Berkeley Street northwards. Sir Cecil Bishop took the first house (afterwards No. 11, Berkeley Square) in 1741. A generation later it became the home of Horace Walpole, who writing to Lady Ossory on October 14th, 1779, announced his arrival:

> I came to town this morning to take possession of Berkeley Square, and am as well pleased as I can be with anything at present.

No. 11 remained in the Walpole family until the 4th Lord Orford lost it in one night of high play at cards to Henry Baring, the banker and father of Lords Revelstoke and Cromer. Lord Orford made his house his last stake, and when Henry Baring rose from the table he was the owner of the house which a few hours before he had entered as a guest – all at the throw of a card. Like all the houses on this side of Berkeley Square and round the corner in Bruton Street it was pulled down in a savage act of demolition in 1937 to make way for that monstrosity in brown brick – Berkeley Square House.

Among the houses demolished in Bruton Street was No. 17, with a fine Palladian front, the birthplace of our present Queen. It belonged to the Earl and Countess of Strathmore, the parents of Lady Elizabeth Bowes-Lyon, now the Queen Mother, who was married from here to the Duke of York, afterwards King George VI. One year later on April 21st, 1926, their first child, Princess Elizabeth, was born in the house. The London branch of the First National City Bank now occupies the site and inside the main entrance is a drawing of 17, Bruton Street with an account of its historic associations.

Luckily, the ugly east side of Berkeley Square is partly veiled by its tall and beautiful plane trees, the most beautiful specimens in London where this tree thrives, shedding its bark and spreading its shade in many squares and streets. The botanists call it *Platanus hybrida* – the London Plane.

The Berkeley Square planes, thirty-three in number, many of them veterans of almost tropical girth and height, are Mayfair's greatest gift to London, and we should remember the man who planted them, Edward Bouverie, who lived two doors away from Horace Walpole at No. 13. The oldest among them are said to date from 1789; they were not planted to commemorate the French Revolution.

One of the few statues in Mayfair stands in the square garden, a scantily draped female figure in marble pouring water from a vase into a basin, but parts of the lady and her basin are missing. She must have been beautiful once because the statue was the gift of the third Marquess of Lansdowne, a great art connoisseur, and was considered by Herbert Spencer to be superior to the *Venus de Milo* albeit the work of a forgotten Victorian sculptor, Alexander Munro.

A charming summer house, half hidden by the trees, stands in the centre of the square, looking like a classical temple or a raised tomb in the seclusion of an ancient and romantic park. In fact it is a pumping station in disguise, supplying water from the tank in the roof – or at least it should do – for the lady down the hill who so captivated Herbert Spencer.

King George III on horseback, the Farmer King incongruously arrayed in classical attire as the Emperor Marcus Aurelius, used to prance on this spot, the gift of his favourite daughter Princess Amelia. The king's statue

– Horace Walpole called it a 'Phidian work' – had to be removed as the rider proved too heavy for his mount, and the horse's legs showed ominous signs of buckling.

Berkeley Square, in spite of the whirligig of traffic and the bare ugly building on its east side, is the most romantic of Mayfair's squares. It is a square of memories – of nightingales, Horace Walpole, Gunter's (we shall come to this Mayfair institution later) and powdered flunkeys taking the air outside the lordly mansions. It looks its best in early May when the plane trees are in feathery leaf, May Fair time. Carnations blossom in men's button holes, women are wearing their spring hats, and even the traffic swirls round at a jaunty pace as if the stream of taxis, private cars, vans, scooters – and buses now – were propelled on a roundabout at a fair.

Several of the original Georgian houses on the west side of the square have escaped destruction, which makes the act of vandalism in destroying the houses opposite seem an even greater crime, and they are now safe under the terms of a Preservation Order (1964).

No. 44, on this side, William Kent's masterpiece, was built for Lady Isabella Finch, a Maid of Honour to Princess Amelia, in 1747. Since it has been renovated and refurnished as the Clermont Club it can claim to be the finest 18th-century house in Mayfair, if not in the whole of London. The Earl of Clermont was the house's second owner, and his portrait hangs in the hall. Lady Clermont, famous for her exquisite dinners, often entertained the Prince Regent here. Walpole knew the house well. 'The staircase at Lady Isabella Finch's', he wrote, 'is as beautiful a piece of scenery and, considering the space, of art as can be imagined.' He used to play at Loo with Lady Finch in the Great Room under the coffered ceiling with its cameos painted by Zucchi, but the card games played there today are rather more exciting. Until it became a club No. 44, Berkeley Square was a private house, the last in the square. Mr Wyndham Clark whose family had lived there since 1874 found the house too large for him and surrendered the lease in 1958.

The house next door, No. 45, used always to be pointed out as one of the last private houses in London which still had the name of its owner engraved on a brass plate on the front door, a custom quite common before the numbering of houses was introduced in 1762.

The house was bought by Lord Clive ('Clive of India') in 1761, and on his death in 1774 – whether he committed suicide or took an overdose of some drug because he was in great pain has never been established – it passed to his son created Earl of Powis, who lived here until his death in 1839. It was this name, 'The Earl of Powis', that was engraved on the small oval brass plate on the front door. It remained, a charming anachronism, until the 4th Earl sold the old family house in 1937 and the historic name plate is now kept at Powis Castle in Montgomeryshire, affixed to the door of Lord Powis's study.

No. 45, Berkeley Square is still maintained as a private house; it was presented to the late Dr Frank Buchman by supporters of Moral Rearmament throughout the world, who also gave furniture and pictures to embellish the magnificent state rooms; it serves now as the social centre of the movement.

Several of the houses on this side have retained their original arrow headed iron railings, springing up into an elegant and graceful arch in front of the entrance with an iron lantern – needed in the days when the streets were unlit – suspended over the steps. On either side of the lantern are the trumpet-shaped link extinguishers used by the link boys for snuffing their burning tapers. The word 'boy' should not be taken literally as it would take a full grown man to reach up to some of them. The 'links', as they were called, long survived the extinction of their torches, and Ralph Nevill writing in 1928 tells us in *Romantic London* that their successor, a well-known figure outside West End houses at balls and parties, was a Mr Richard Trebilcock, known as 'Happy', who was the most celebrated linkman in London. He wore a glossy silk hat and red waistcoat and carrying a square lantern with a candle in it spent half the night opening and shutting the doors of motor cars as his predecessors had lighted the elegants of another age as they stepped from their chaises and sedan chairs.

Luckily many examples of the fine 18th-century iron work have survived in Mayfair, especially in the streets to the west of Berkeley Square, where the proportion of Georgian houses is higher than elsewhere. Two famous streets lead off the west side of Berkeley Square, Hill Street and Charles Street, once lined with large private houses, but mostly clubs or business premises now. The Guards Club at No. 16, Charles Street used to be the sumptuous town house of the Hon. Mrs Ronald Greville, the large ground-floor rooms built round a courtyard; and on the opposite side stands Dartmouth House, now the English Speaking Union, an even grander house rebuilt regardless of cost by Lord Revelstoke in 1890.

We want to walk down the west side of Berkeley Square into Fitzmaurice Place, and we must try to visualise how this corner of Mayfair looked when Lansdowne House stood here in all its glory.

Robert Adam was faced with a tricky problem in 1762 when he began building Lansdowne House as he could not site it on the south side of the square because of the original clause in Lord Berkeley's agreement with the Duke of Devonshire. But he could use the open space as a garden, and he adroitly placed the house at right angles to it on the site of some stables in Bolton Row at the end of Curzon Street. The Earl of Bute was its first owner, but after a brief stay he sold the house in an uncompleted state to the Earl of Shelburne, created Marquess of Lansdowne in 1784.

Lansdowne House was famous for its works of art – the antique statuary collected by Gavin Hamilton for the first Marquess and the Old Masters by the third Marquess. It was famous too for its brilliant political gatherings, and the apartments, when thrown open for receptions, were said to hold a greater number of people than those of any other private house. The Grand Gallery with its famous antique statues and Old Masters was 100 feet long.

One of the last great social events held at Lansdowne House was the wedding reception for Harold Macmillan when he married Lady Dorothy Cavendish on April 21st, 1920. The Duke and Duchess of Devonshire, the bride's parents, assembled the cream of London society, and among the guests who toasted the young couple's health after the ceremony at St Margaret's, Westminster, were Queen Alexandra and her daughter Princess Victoria, Prince Albert, later King George VI, and the Duke of Connaught. The Macmillans, not to be outdone by this impressive array, paraded their famous authors, led by Thomas Hardy who paid his last visit to London for the wedding, and wore his Order of Merit.

The reception was held at Lansdowne House, and not Devonshire House, the home of the bride's parents, as this famous Piccadilly mansion had been sold only a week before. So Lord Lansdowne, being the bride's grandfather, lent his house next door.

High taxation, death duties and the post-war slump were taking their toll all over Mayfair and agents' bill-boards 'To Let' and 'For Sale' plastered the empty houses in Berkeley Square as elsewhere in the West End. Lansdowne House escaped the fate of Devonshire House: instead of being demolished it was let to a rich tenant, Gordon Selfridge, who paid the enormous sum of £5000 a year rent for it.

Selfridge was then at the apex of his fantastic career, with his wealth pouring in from the cash registers of his mammoth store in Oxford

Street. During his tenancy the Adam rooms of Lansdowne House became the scene of glittering parties in the new idiom of the nineteen twenties, at which the Dolly Sisters, scintillating with diamonds, led the guests in the Black Bottom and the Charleston to the wail of saxophones. Mayfair had entered on its post-war phase culminating in the antics of the Bright Young People at the end of the decade.

Monsieur Paul Cambon, the distinguished French ambassador who had negotiated the *Entente Cordiale* with Lord Lansdowne, revisited London in the mid-'twenties and, wishing to see his old friend, called at Lansdowne House which he knew well from the old days having often attended grand receptions there. As he drove up, the house with its large garden stretching along the south side of Berkeley Square looked familiar enough, but when he handed in his card the butler informed him that the Marquess of Lansdowne no longer lived there, and the house was let to Mr Gordon Selfridge.

'*Cela m'a donné un coup*', the veteran French ambassador remarked wistfully afterwards.

Lansdowne House still stands, but in a sadly mutilated form. Its front has been cut off to a depth of 40 feet and the main façade rebuilt on the truncated building shorn of its two low graceful wings and with two storeys added. This drastic surgery was performed in 1935 to allow Curzon Street to be continued into Berkeley Square, a threat which still hangs over Mayfair. Two rooms decorated by Robert Adam in the front of the house were salvaged and transported to America; the First Drawing Room with decorations by Cipriani, Zucchi and Perfetti has been reconstructed in the Pennsylvania Museum of Art in Philadelphia, and the Dining Room in the Metropolitan Museum of Art in New York. A fine marble chimney-piece, removed from Lansdowne House at this time, was presented to the London Library and adorns the Prevost Room. The Lansdowne Club now occupies Robert Adam's chopped-up building.

The garden of Lansdowne House and the garden of Devonshire House (famous for its elms and its statuary) were adjoining, and between them ran old Lansdowne Passage, connecting Berkeley Street with Curzon Street. The passage was a right of way belonging to Lord Lansdowne who had to close it one day in the year to maintain his rights. It was below the level of the ground which made it a favourite place for murders in fiction, and perhaps in fact too, and was approached down a few steps from Berkeley Street; there were also steps at the Curzon Street end. An upright bar was placed at its entrance after a highwayman made a daring raid in Piccadilly and galloping down Berkeley Street, then narrow and unpaved, escaped through Lansdowne Passage into Curzon Street and back to Piccadilly. Thomas Grenville, Pitt's Foreign Minister, lived in Bolton Street and saw the escaping highwayman ride past at full gallop. Lansdowne Passage still exists with steps leading down to it, but it is no longer a right of way, and has been turned into an emergency exit for the May Fair Hotel.

Sir Richard Grosvenor, 'the great builder', should have a statue erected to him in Mayfair. Thanks to his wise planning, the street pattern of the north-west section of Mayfair has hardly changed since he laid out, in 1725, the great square which bears his name, and fitted it into a grid of straight streets crossing each other at right angles.

Looking at John Rocque's map of this part of Mayfair published in 1747 it is surprising to see how little the plan of the streets has altered; it can still be used for finding one's way about, for not only are the streets still as Sir Richard Grosvenor planned them but their names have remained the same, even those of back streets and mews – like Adam's Mews and Three Kings Yard. Rocque gives the name Three Kings Court, but corrects it in a later edition, and David Street is meant for Davies Street.

Sir Richard started with many advantages over other ground landlords in Mayfair, the most important being that he owned so much land and could plan on the grand scale, though, as we shall see, his idea of making St George's Church, Hanover Square, on the east side of his estate, into an architectural feature at the end of a long vista failed through lack of co-operation on the part of his neighbours.

The Oxford or Tyburn Road formed the northern border of his estate. Tyburn brook enclosed it from the east, it adjoined the Berkeley lands on the south, and on the west it was divided from Hyde Park by Tyburn Lane, as Park Lane was then called. In all he owned an estate of nearly one hundred acres in Mayfair, part of the dowry of agricultural land which his mother, Mary Davies, brought into the Grosvenor family when she married Sir Thomas Grosvenor at St Clement Danes in the Strand on October 10th, 1677. The child bride – she was only thirteen when she married Sir Thomas who was 21 – was the great-grand-niece of Hugh Audley, a thrifty moneylender, who died 'infinitely rich' in 1662, but without issue. North Audley Street, South Audley Street and Audley Square are named after him.

Hugh Audley's estate which eventually devolved on Mary Davies consisted of a large part of the old manor of Eye, called the Manor of

Ebury, once the property of the Abbots of Westminster – a huge expanse of agricultural land stretching down to the Thames at Millbank.

Her fields, however, were of potential value only because they had to be developed, and her husband (whose property they automatically became on marriage according to the law of the day) was actually far richer than his wife in terms of ready cash. He had mines in the north. Also, her match with a Cheshire baronet was a considerable step up in the social ladder for the young girl.

The Grosvenor–Davies marriage took place eleven years after the Great Fire of London. Within two generations an entirely new part of town – Mayfair – was built largely on Mary Davies's fields north of Piccadilly, which helped to replace the destroyed City as a new residential part of London. To her fortunate descendants the match brought immense wealth and a steady rise in the peerage until Mary Davies's great-great-great-grandson, Hugh Lupus, 3rd Marquess of Westminster, was created Duke of Westminster by Queen Victoria in 1874 and married Constance, the daughter of the Queen's great friend, Harriet Duchess of Sutherland. His grandson, the second Duke, was said to have an income of £1,000 a day before 1914: he died in 1953, the richest man in England, owning ninety acres in Mayfair and one hundred and eighty acres in Belgravia, Mary Davies's erstwhile fields. His property was assessed at about £18 million on which estate duty of £12 million was levied.

Mary Davies's father, Alexander Davies, died of the plague in 1665, and was buried in the churchyard of St Margaret's, Westminster. His raised tomb can still be seen through the railings by the pavement near the north door of the Abbey – the only gravestone still above ground. When the churchyard was levelled and the graves turfed over at the end of the last century the first Duke of Westminster asked for it to be left standing out of respect for his Davies ancestors: their name is perpetuated in Mayfair in Davies Street.

Alexander Davies's wife, who was born with the prophetic surname of Dukeson, is also buried in St Margaret's. She survived her husband by more than half a century and married secondly John Tregonwell. She was an intensely ambitious woman, and at first betrothed her heiress daughter, Mary, at the age of eight, to Charles, the ten-year old son and heir of Lord Berkeley of Stratton, obviously with an eye on the neighbouring Berkeley lands to the south-east of the Tyburn, hoping to see her daughter installed one day at Berkeley House as the future Lady Berkeley.

As part of the marriage contract Lord Berkeley agreed to deposit

£5,000 with Mary's parents and also to settle £3,000 in land on his son when he married his child bride. But Lord Berkeley was unable to fulfil his side of the bargain, and the engagement was broken off. It is interesting to speculate what might have happened had the two estates been joined by this Berkeley–Davies match, which would have brought almost all of Mayfair under one landlord. Certainly the Dowager Lady Berkeley would have had a good deal to say in its development.

The first generation of Mayfair ground landlords, like Lord Berkeley of Stratton, Sir Thomas Bond and the Earl of Dover, who developed their land on the northern side of Piccadilly, were men of the Restoration, champions of King Charles II.

Sir Richard Grosvenor, the eldest son of Sir Thomas Grosvenor and Mary Davies, came of age in 1700 and belonged to the new century. When Queen Anne died he spent no time in regretting the Stuarts. Following in his father's footsteps, he represented the City of Chester in the House of Commons, and being a Whig in politics threw himself wholeheartedly behind the Hanoverian succession. He had property to develop, houses to sell, and his eye was fixed firmly on the future.

His full-length portrait hangs in Chester Town Hall and a copy among the family pictures in the Grosvenor Estate Office in Davies Street. We see a burly north countryman, fashionably but not foppishly dressed with ruffs and a lace cravat, his full-bottomed wig frothing over his shoulders. We can imagine him striding over the muddy building sites of his estate, pegging out the land, and then sitting down to an alfresco luncheon in a large tent with his tenants and workmen, and solemnly naming the new streets to the accompaniment of bumper toasts.

In the *Daily Journal* of July 12th, 1725, we read:

> The several new streets designed in Grosvenor Building lying between New Bond Street and Hyde Park were lately particularly named; upon which occasion Sir Richard Grosvenor, Bt., gave a very splendid entertainment to his tenants and others concerned in these buildings. . . . There is now building a Square called Grosvenor Square, which for its largeness and beauty will far exceed any yet made in and about London.

He not only had wide acres on which to lay out his estate, but its position was superb. His land was on the plateau south of the Oxford Road – Londoners had never lived so high up before – and it adjoined

47

open country. Healthy surroundings were now an important consideration with the horrors of the plague still a very vivid memory.

He started his building operations by laying out Grosvenor Square six
acres in extent (a square in the geometrical sense of the word) with a
gilded statue by Van Nost of the reigning monarch in the centre, showing
him mounted on a horse and dressed as a Roman Emperor. He paid this
compliment to King George I (it cost him £262. 10s.) even before the
first houses were built.

The Jacobites regarded the statue as a provocation, and damaged it,
as we know from the bills which have been preserved for 'watching ye
figure' and 'mending the statue of ye King and Horse – a new sword and
Truncheon, Putting a leg on, Guilding the same and other places'.

The Jacobites also circulated an apparently harmless rhyme about the
King's statue.

> *King Charles's black nag being tired of the Town*
> *From fair Charing Cross one evening stole down*
> *And trotting along towards the fields for fresh air*
> *He spied a strange beast up in Grosvenor Square.*

Some thirty years later the 'beast' was compared to a piece of gingerbread in a greengrocer's stall. But this was not Jacobite propaganda –
merely a description of the statue as it looked when the bushes and trees
planted by Sir Richard Grosvenor had grown up around it. The statue
vanished about 100 years ago, but part of the pedestal was still visible
among the trees before the last war.

Sir Richard Grosvenor wanted to attract the fashionable world to his
estate, and in his show-piece, Grosvenor Square, he built larger terrace
houses than any yet seen in London, with gardens at the back and cottages
in the mews for coachmen and upper servants. But other noble landlords
were building in Mayfair. A few years earlier the South Sea Bubble had
burst and fortunes had been lost. Dukes had become paupers. But money
had also been won. The King's two German mistresses, raised to the
peerage as the Duchess of Kendal and the Countess of Darlington (the
skinny one nicknamed 'The Maypole' and the fat one 'The Elephant and
Castle') had made fortunes out of the South Sea Bubble and the sale of
honours. In 1727 the King died, and both harridans had to leave St James's
Palace. 'The Maypole' cast her eyes on Mayfair, and after taking the
Duke of St Albans's house in Old Bond Street for a year, moved into
Grosvenor Square in 1728. So Sir Richard had his first Duchess – actually

5. CLARENDON HOUSE. Clarendon House, later called Albemarle House, stood between Dover Street and Old Bond Street, looking down St James's to the Palace. Built by Hugh May for Lord Clarendon in 1665, it was demolished twenty years later. (Crace Collection, British Museum)

6. BURLINGTON HOUSE. The garden of old Burlington House stretched far back into present-day Mayfair. Trinity Chapel on the left marks the line of Conduit Street, the site of the Westbury Hotel today. (Crace Collection, British Museum)

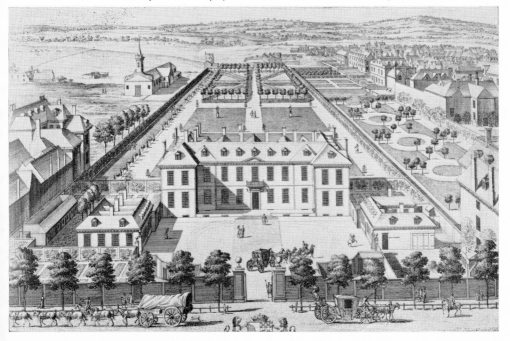

7. LANSDOWNE HOUSE. Lansdowne House (*right*) was built by Robert Adam for the Earl of Bute who sold it to the first Marquess of Lansdowne. Its large garden covered the southern side of Berkeley Square. Much altered, Lansdowne House is now a club. (London Museum)

8. LANSDOWNE PASSAGE. Lansdowne Passage connected Berkeley Street with Curzon Street and ran below ground level between the gardens of Devonshire House and Lansdowne House. (London Museum)

the only Duchess who took a house in Grosvenor Square during his lifetime, though many others were to follow her there.

'The Maypole' took a lease of a house on the south side of Grosvenor Square, which still stands, numbered 43. She occupied it until her death in 1743, outliving the King by sixteen years and she was, no doubt, reminded of him every time she looked out of her front windows and saw his gilded statue, but whether this memento of her late lord brought pleasant memories we do not know.

Sir Richard's other tenants on this side – the first to be completed – were mostly fellow Members of Parliament: Henry Bromley, M.P. for Cambridgeshire; Frederic Frankland, M.P. for Thirsk; Oliver St George, M.P. for Dungannon in Ireland; Charles Calvert, M.P. for Surrey, afterwards Lord Baltimore, the hereditary proprietor of Maryland.

Another row of M.P.s lived on the north side of the square, including the notorious John Aislabie, the Chancellor of the Exchequer, who was expelled from the House of Commons after the exposure of the South Sea Bubble scandal, and committed to the Tower. His house (which he bought after his fall) looked directly across at the Duchess of Kendal's. It seems almost as if Members of Parliament – and the King's mistress – were the only ones able to afford a house in Grosvenor Square at this time. No fewer than 462 M.P.s were known to have held South Sea stock. No slur fell on Sir Richard himself, however. He rose high in favour at Court, and in the new reign performed the ceremonial duty of Cup Bearer at the coronation of King George II. He died in 1732, having lived to see his great square and most of the neighbouring streets well on the way to completion, and leaving to his descendants the agreeable task of reaping 'the golden acres'.

Of Sir Richard's half a hundred four-storey houses in Grosvenor Square only two remain today, No. 43, where 'The Maypole' lived, now divided into two flats with an extra storey added, and its neighbour, No. 44 (originally 39)[1], the last private house in the square.

Throughout the 18th century King George I's gilded statue stood in the centre of the circular formal garden planted with dwarf trees and patterned with an arabesque of walks; and if we imagine the two surviving 18th-century houses in their original state repeated with slight variations on all four sides we can reconstruct the square of red brick houses as it used to look at this time. Its size must have seemed tremendous – a contem-

---

[1] Grosvenor Square was renumbered in 1888.

porary writer calls it 'the most magnificent square in the whole Town'[1] – and the sense of space was further increased by the expanse of roadway between the houses and the circular garden, deserted except for an occasional coach or sedan chair, with perhaps a cowman driving his beasts across the uneven cobblestones.

No. 44 Grosvenor Square on the south side is occasionally opened to the public by its owner, Lady Illingworth. The interior, as one might expect in a square so long the most fashionable in London, has been altered and embellished to suit the tastes of succeeding owners. In 1960 a large mural was revealed behind the panelling in the upstairs Drawing Room, arousing a great deal of interest at the time and hailed as an important art discovery.

Lady Illingworth had always heard that a 'fresco thought to be by Hogarth' was hidden behind the panelling in her pale blue drawing room, but had never satisfied her curiosity as it meant taking down mirrors and pictures, and causing a general upheaval in such a beautiful room. But when some repair work was being carried out in her house she thought it was the right moment to see if the story of the fresco was true, and the workmen took down one of the panels. When it was removed – it was of light material fixed on wooden joists – the head of a man in a full-bottomed wig looked out from the wall, and it was quite obvious that there was more 'fresco' on either side. So in the course of the next few days down came a second, a third and a fourth panel, each time disclosing another figure until the theme of the painting was revealed – a *conversazione* on a balcony between eight figures divided into three groups.

The man in the wig who appeared first is seen to be talking to two Polish noblemen in national costume, an eager youth is leaning over the shoulder of a flower girl, whispering sweet nothings in her ear, a strawberry girl proudly balances a basket of luscious fruit on her head ignoring a wild looking man who wants to buy, and belonging to no group the enigmatic figure of a man with rather a surly expression thought to be a self-portrait of William Kent, who often put himself in his painting. For Kent is now thought to be the artist of the large work, which is painted in oils directly on the wall, and therefore not a fresco but a mural. Kent is responsible for a similar balcony scene over the King's Staircase at Kensington.

The painted wall was covered up as recently as 1929 when the late Lord Illingworth, the husband of the present owner, bought the house

[1] *London in Miniature*, 1755.

and had the drawing room redecorated by Sir Charles Allom in the fashionable Adam style with egg-shell blue panelling as a setting for de Laszlo's portrait of his wife. The panelling was placed over the mural with extreme care and it emerged thirty-one years later without a scratch on it, its rich reds and blues as fresh as the day it was painted, probably at the time the house was built for the first tenant, Oliver St George, M.P., in 1725. The mural originally formed part of the hall decoration, the figures looking over the balustrade to give the impression of height and space. At a later date the staircase was taken out of the hall and the ceiling lowered: as a result of the alterations the mural became the east wall of the enlarged upstairs drawing room.

After the death of Mrs St George in 1747 the house passed through the hands of several owners – Lord Harcourt, Lord Scarborough, Sir Edward Dering, Lord Aylesford – until it was bought by Dudley Ryder, the first Earl of Harrowby, in 1804. During his lifetime – he was Secretary of State for Foreign Affairs and Lord President of the Council – all the leading statesmen of the day came to the house – it being customary in those days of spacious living for the Cabinet to meet for dinner at members' houses in rotation. The Cabinet dinner was usually held at Lord Harrowby's house on a Wednesday, and on the occasion of two dinners – Wednesday June 21st, 1815 and Wednesday February 23rd, 1820 – stirring events happened (or perhaps it would be more accurate to say in respect of the dinner on February 23rd, 1820, nearly happened).

On Wednesday June 21st, 1815, the Cabinet, presided over by Lord Liverpool, met for dinner in a state of great uncertainty, not knowing what to believe – the rumour that Napoleon had won a decisive victory over the Allies outside Brussels, or the garbled story brought to Downing Street that morning by Nathan Rothschild, the head of the London branch of the family, who had received the news from his courier service that Napoleon had been defeated by Wellington near a small village with the unfamiliar name of Waterloo.

The betting in the St James's Street clubs was on Napoleon, and the members of the Cabinet who sat round Lord Harrowby's dining table expected the worst. At about 10 o'clock – it was still light, being midsummer – a tremendous cheer was heard outside the house and a few moments later the door of the dining room burst open and in dashed a dishevelled-looking young officer in a scarlet tunic, Major the Hon. Henry Percy, the Duke of Wellington's A.D.C., who had come post haste from Brussels with the Duke's despatch to Earl Bathurst, Secretary of State for War, announcing the great victory.[1]

The cheering outside the house woke up Lord Harrowby's second daughter, Mary, who crept down the staircase in her nightdress and, looking over the banisters, saw Percy dash in, brandishing the despatch. Born in 1801, she married Admiral Saurin and, living to be a hundred, passed on her eye-witness account of the historic scene to her great-grand-nephew, Lord Harrowby, who in his turn has passed on her story to Lady Illingworth.

The second Cabinet dinner, on Wednesday February 23rd, 1820, would have ended in bloodshed and riot if all had gone according to plan. A gang of desperadoes led by a visionary, Arthur Thistlewood, who knew of the Cabinet dinner, planned to force their way into Lord Harrowby's house. One of them was to gain entry first by pretending he had important papers to deliver, and the rest would then rush in and murder the whole Cabinet as they sat at dinner. This bloody deed accomplished and with the heads of Lord Sidmouth, the hated Home Secretary, and Lord Castlereagh in sacks specially brought for the purpose, their next objective was to proclaim the 'Provisional Government of the People' on the steps of the Mansion House, exhibiting the severed heads of the tyrants to, it was hoped, a grateful citizenry.

Such was the plot hatched in the loft above a stable in a cul-de-sac off the Edgware Road called Cato Street, which has given its name to the conspiracy. But by chance Lord Harrowby was riding in the park that morning and was warned by an old family retainer who knew of the plot.

The Duke of Wellington, the Master of the Ordnance, was a member of the Cabinet and advised Lord Liverpool that the dinner should be held as planned, and that soldiers disguised as manservants should be posted inside the hall to overpower the conspirators. However, the other members of the Cabinet did not much relish the idea of being potted at over their soup and fish, so the dinner was cancelled but Lord Harrowby's servants were not told of the change of plan.

By chance the Archbishop of York, who lived two doors away, was giving a large dinner party that evening, so that one of Thistlewood's spies was able to report back that guests were arriving in Grosvenor Square as expected. The police (the soldiers who were to accompany

[1] The Waterloo Despatch is on view in the museum of the Record Office in Chancery Lane. The draft, with corrections in Wellington's hand, is kept in the library at Apsley House.

9. 17, BRUTON STREET. No. 17, Bruton Street, Berkeley Square, the birthplace of Queen Elizabeth II. From a watercolour drawing by J. Richardson (1810) in the British Museum.

10. 45, BERKELEY SQUARE. No. 45, Berkeley Square was the home of Clive of India who died here. For many years the brass plate on the front door bore the name of the Earl of Powis, his descendant.

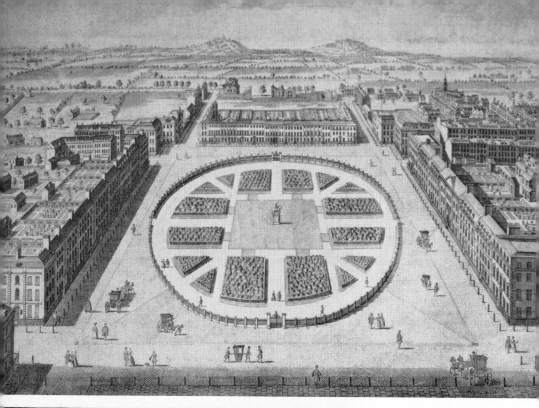

11. GROSVENOR SQUARE.
Sir Richard Grosvenor laid
out the square which bears
his name in 1725, and it remained the most fashionable
part of London for 200
years.

12. SIR RICHARD GROS-
VENOR, Bt. Sir Richard Grosvenor, the 'Great Builder',
was the son of Mary Davies
who married Sir Thomas
Grosvenor. His portrait
hangs in Chester Town Hall,
and a copy in the Grosvenor
Estate Office, Davies Street.

them lost their way) raided the loft and arrested most of the conspirators after a sharp fight which resulted in the death of a constable, who was run through the body with a bayonet. Thistlewood and the ringleaders were publicly hanged outside Newgate Prison after a sensational trial. Five were transported to Australia, one of them named Strange became a much esteemed constable in the Bathurst District, and was nicknamed the 'Cato Street Chief', obviously making the most of his connection with the plot: he lived to a great age, and founded a large family; his descendants must be alive today.

Back at Grosvenor Square the chef was not told until 8 o'clock that the dinner was cancelled and that Lord and Lady Harrowby were to dine quietly in their rooms. He was so infuriated – he was a temperamental Frenchman – that he stamped on his white chef's hat and threw all his carefully prepared dishes for the Cabinet dinner into the fire. The kitchen where he made this Gallic gesture is below stairs in the cavernous basement and is still in use, joined by a hundred-yard vaulted tunnel to the main kitchens at the back of the house in Adam's Row.

Sir Richard Grosvenor's austere looking houses, of which No. 43 and 44 are the only examples left, suited the taste of the 18th-century noblemen for whom they were built, but not the Victorians who considered the houses too plain. However, change came slowly to Grosvenor Square. Gas lighting introduced in Pall Mall in 1807 was opposed for years by the diehard residents of the older generation who, proud of their flambeaux, refused to adopt the new invention, considering it vulgar and unsuitable for their aristocratic square. Tom Moore wrote:

> . . . *In Grosvenor's lordly Square,*
> *That last impregnable redoubt,*
> *Where guarded with patrician care,*
> *Primeval error still holds out.*
>
> *Where never gleam of gas must dare*
> *'gainst ancient darkness to revolt*
> *Nor smooth Macadam hope to spare*
> *The Dowagers one single jolt;*
>
> *Where, far too stately and sublime*
> *To profit by the lights of time,*
> *Let intellect march how it will,*
> *They stick to oil and watchmen still.*

Gas lighting was not introduced finally until 1842 when the houses began to change too. If Grosvenor Square had gone out of fashion at this time the chances are that it would have come down to us an almost perfect 18th-century example like Bedford Square in Bloomsbury. But it became increasingly fashionable and during the rest of the century one house after the other was either refronted, the height raised by the addition of an upper storey, the elegant Georgian front door and fanlight masked by a ponderous Victorian portico, the glazing bars removed from the windows or the whole house pulled down and rebuilt like No. 41 which belonged to Lord Nunburnholme, the shipping magnate, who as Charles Wilson was M.P. for Hull. He built an entirely new mansion on the site of the old Georgian house, with a pink marble staircase and sumptuous rooms at the cost of £60,000 in 1885. The house served as the Library and exhibition rooms of the American Embassy after the war, and was pulled down in the early 1960s when its staircase was torn out and sold in the King's Road, Chelsea.

Even the 'Waterloo House', No. 44, did not escape, and its brown brick façade was 'improved' by the addition of a bow window to the famous dining room on the right of the front door, now the morning room. The Hon. H. Dudley Ryder, later the 4th Earl of Harrowby, wrote to his father on November 28th, 1877:

> . . . rode by Grosvenor Square this morning to see how the work progressed. They are just beginning the brickwork of the Bow, having put in the iron girder, and now probably that will soon be done, for brickwork is very rapid. The new windows upstairs are in. . . .

No mention is made of alterations inside the house, but probably the staircase was taken out at this time, and the upstairs drawing room enlarged to include the mural. Luckily the cast-iron arrow-headed railings with their elegant lamp-holders and trumpet-shaped link extinguishers were left in place. The ground rent at that time was £350 p.a. and the rent £700 p.a.

Visitors to No. 44 are surprised to find that the french windows of the back morning room open out on a long stone flagged garden ornamented with a classical temple at the far end, and with statues standing in niches along the wall. To sit here in the summer among the flowers listening to the cooing of the pigeons in the trees is to forget one is in the heart of the West End. At night the garden can be floodlit.

Two other houses in the square have survived, but they were both rebuilt in the last century: No. 4 on the east side, the Italian Embassy; and No. 38 on the south, the Indonesian Embassy. No. 4 used to be the town house of the Fitzwilliam family for many years and was rebuilt on a sumptuous scale by the 6th Earl, who left a fortune of nearly £3 million in 1902. It became the Italian Embassy in 1933 when Count Grandi embellished it with works of art from Italy; the large rooms *en suite* upstairs have the grandeur of a Roman palace. Its fellow survivor, No. 38, with its stucco front and portico, is typical of the style in which the Victorians rebuilt Sir Richard Grosvenor's houses. For over 130 years it was the town house of the Gough-Calthorpe family.

Many houses remained in the same family from one generation to another. No. 27 on the west side held the record. Anthony Ashley Cooper, 4th Earl of Shaftesbury, was the house's first owner in 1732, and his descendant, the 7th Earl, the famous philanthropist, lived here until his death in 1885. The 'Waterloo' house belonged to the Harrowby family for over a century until Mary, Countess of Harrowby, widow of the 3rd Earl, left in 1908. The next tenant was the Dowager Duchess of Devonshire, who had to move finally from Devonshire House on the death of the Duke. The bell indicator in the stone flagged passage in the basement still refers to 'Her Grace's Room', the Red Room on the first floor. She carried out large-scale alterations in the house, installing its first bathroom, but lived here only one year. She had a long and memorable life. As the young German born Lady Mandeville she first attracted the attention of Queen Victoria and Prince Albert, and then as Duchess of Manchester she became the confidante of statesmen. She died at No. 44 in 1911.

Grosvenor Square emerged from the first World War much changed. Many of the old families had moved out and as elsewhere in Mayfair house agents' boards began to appear, and at the time of the slump half the houses were empty. In 1931 the Grosvenor Estate started its rebuilding plan, replacing the old family mansions by blocks of neo-Georgian luxury flats of seven and eight storeys, with the aim of eventually making the square an architectural unit again as in Sir Richard Grosvenor's day.

The north, west and southern sides had been partly rebuilt when the second World War broke out, and the Americans, who had already set up their Embassy at No. 1 Grosvenor Square, took over several of the new blocks for their armed forces. General Eisenhower established his headquarters on the northern side diagonally across from the Embassy, and Admiral Stark housed the naval mission next door; and there were other military offices and installations elsewhere in the square, which soon became known as 'Eisenhower Platz'.

After the war Grosvenor Square, because of its associations with the United States, was chosen as the site of the memorial to President Franklin D. Roosevelt. The Duke of Westminster donated the land, and the old garden, which had become a wilderness, was laid out in a formal pattern with a broad walk leading to the statue, the work of Sir William Reid Dick. This was unveiled by Mrs Eleanor Roosevelt in the presence of King George VI in 1948. Sixty-six fine old trees had to be felled, and now with its 'Keep off the Grass' signs and its brick red geraniums lining the long stone walk leading to the statue, it has become a municipal, not a 'square' garden. It would have been wiser to have placed the memorial to this great friend of Britain in the centre of the square where George I's statue used to stand, and not to have cut down so many fine old trees.

In the late 1950s the whole western side of the square, where there were many old and derelict houses in various styles which had survived the bombing, was levelled to the ground to make way for Eero Saarinen's white and gold United States Embassy surmounted by an enormous eagle, its wings outspread. The choice of contemporary architecture for the new Embassy meant abandoning the plan to reconstruct the square entirely in neo-Georgian, but Saarinen's long and comparatively low building does not upset the proportions of the square and in fact sets off the more conventional style of the red brick neo-Georgian blocks with their white facings. The former United States Embassy, Nos. 1–3, is now Macdonald House, the Canadian High Commissioner's Office.

The work of transforming Sir Richard Grosvenor's square, or what the Victorians left of it, is still not complete. The south side has been rebuilt at each end only and, following the demolition of the four Victorian houses in the centre in 1962 where there is now a gap, three houses belonging to the old square still remain: No. 38, No. 43 and No. 44.

The Ministry of Housing and Local Government rejected an appeal in 1961 to save No. 44, the 'Waterloo House', from being pulled down, on the grounds that its exterior and interior had lost a great deal of their original Georgian character and its retention was holding up the redevelopment of the square, so when its lease runs out, unless the unexpected happens, it will vanish with the other two for which no appeal had been made, though the lease of No. 38 does not run out until 2008.

When the time comes for No. 44 to be pulled down, not only an original Georgian house of historic and artistic distinction will be demolished, but the last example in the square of a house where for nearly 250 years the old traditions and style have been and continue to be kept up.

No. 9, Grosvenor Square, in the north-east corner, is also a Georgian house, but it belongs more properly to Brook Street, and as it does not interfere with the rebuilding plans will probably be spared, especially as it has been reconstructed inside. If Nos. 43 and 44 do disappear No. 9 will remain to show future generations what the houses in the square once looked like. A plaque erected by the Colonial Dames of America recalls that it was the home of John Adams, the first American Minister at the Court of St James's, from May 1785–March 1788, and from here his daughter Abigail was married to Colonel William Stephens Smith, the first Secretary to the Legation and an officer in the revolutionary army on Washington's staff. This house was John Adams's private residence and the Legation offices were in Hertford Street.

While John Adams was in residence in the north-east corner of the square, Lord North was living at No. 50 in the opposite corner. One wonders if they ever met. John Adams, who liked to refer to himself as 'John Yankee', felt ill at ease in London, but chiefly on account of his own government who did not allow him enough money to 'keep up a style of living like other foreign ministers', a common complaint among his successors who, until the 1930s when Ambassador Joseph Kennedy moved the Embassy to No. 1, Grosvenor Square, had to make do with shabby, ill-lit, badly furnished offices at 123, Victoria Street.

At the end of the last century Lord North's house belonged to the Duchess of Marlborough, and her son Lord Randolph Churchill lived here for three years until his death at No. 50 on January 24th, 1895. Sir Winston Churchill described in *My Early Life* how he was summoned from a neighbouring house in the early morning and 'ran in the darkness across Grosvenor Square, then lapped with snow' to be present at his father's end. By a strange coincidence his own death occurred on the same day seventy years later. *1965*

No. 47, Grosvenor Square, now rebuilt as flats, used to have a racquets court at the back approached by a separate entrance in Carlos Place. This added refinement to a Mayfair home dated from the nineteen-thirties and was built by Major Stephen Courtauld, who lived at No. 47 between the wars. The racquets court is now the Ohana Gallery, specialising in French Impressionists and modern art.

So many famous men and women have lived in Grosvenor Square that one can pay an endless round of imaginary calls. On the east side No. 2 was William Beckford's house and during his tenancy Sir William and Lady Hamilton lived there with Nelson as their guest. The Earl of Coventry lived at No. 3 before he moved to his new house in Piccadilly in 1764, overlooking at the back the old fair-ground. Lady Cunard lived at No. 7 – 'the most original of hostesses who could bring forth the hidden qualities of the most intractable material,' writes Harold Acton in his *Memoirs of an Aesthete*. One never knew who would be present and her guests were amusingly incongruous. She gave up her house during the war and went to live at the Dorchester Hotel, where she died. But her spirit still hovers over Grosvenor Square as her ashes were scattered in the garden. Lord Lytton, the author of *The Last Days of Pompeii*, lived at No. 12, the last of his many houses in Mayfair, earlier the home of John Aislabie, the erring Chancellor of the Exchequer. It was also the home of John Pierpont Morgan, father and son. But all these houses have vanished. The Europa Hotel now occupies the site of Nos. 10–14, with its main entrance in Duke Street.

It is only a few steps along Brook Street to the Grosvenor Estate Office at the corner of Davies Street where the London estate of the Duke of Westminster is administered under the watching eyes of generations of the Grosvenor family. In the hall in a place of honour hangs the portrait of the mother of them all, Mary Davies, after Michael Dahl, showing her as the widowed Lady Grosvenor, and nearby the portrait of her eldest son, Sir Richard, 'the great builder'.

Sir Richard Grosvenor certainly would have been pleased to see how soon his square – after a quiet beginning – became so fashionable. Did not Arthur Dasent, the historian of Grosvenor Square who went to endless trouble to trace the names of all the residents, describe Sir Richard's lordly square as 'strewn with the strawberry leaves and blue ribbons of the Garter'? And it is still mainly a residential square today, which cannot be said of either Berkeley Square or Hanover Square.

Sir Richard Grosvenor had one disappointment, however. He planned Grosvenor Street to be one of the show streets of London. Here were fine houses on either side, each with gracefully carved doorways flanked by fluted pilasters. It was the broadest street on his estate, which it crossed from end to end starting as Upper Grosvenor Street at the Park end, and leading to St George's Church – at least, that is what he planned.

If we stand on one of the islands in Grosvenor Street and look eastwards we can see St George's steeple just peeping over the roof tops, but the classical portico, though directly in line with the axis of Grosvenor Street and Upper Grosvenor Street beyond, is concealed. Sir Richard Grosvenor intended St George's on its slight eminence between New Bond Street and Regent Street to be seen at the end of the long vista which would have been a truly noble view from Park Lane. The church was built some years before he laid out his estate, so he could align his street plan accordingly. But unfortunately his land ended at the Tyburn, and across the boundary lay the City's Conduit Mead Estate. The Tyburn flows about thirty yards to the west of New Bond Street, and it is just at this point that the houses on the south side of Grosvenor Street bulge forward, masking the front of St George's, and the bulge grows larger on the far side of New Bond Street in Maddox Street.

There was no coordination between the two estates, and the houses were allowed to be built out of line at the far end of Grosvenor Street. It is interesting to note that this short stretch of Grosvenor Street used to be known as Maddox Street too, a continuation of present-day Maddox Street. The King's Arms Tavern bulked large at the corner in the 1740s, in vulgar contrast to the elegant houses built by Sir Richard Grosvenor on his estate. The houses which stand on the site of this vanished pub and the buildings in Maddox Street blot out what should have been one of the finest views in London – the graceful colonnaded façade of St George's seen at the end of a long avenue of fine houses. Town planners and street wideners, so eager to pull down old buildings in the interest of traffic, should be set to work here to give to London the vista that Sir Richard planned.

Hanover Square once so fashionable has suffered the same fate as so many other London squares further east. It has lost its fine old buildings and the 'quality' has deserted it. The decline started well over a hundred years ago, soon after the building of Nash's Regent Street which with Oxford Street brought commercial London to the doorstep almost of the elegant residents, causing an exodus from this north-east corner of Mayfair. First the old red brick houses, of which only two or three remain, were taken over by learned societies like the Zoological Society, which established itself at No. 11, and the Royal College of Chemistry at No. 16.

Then it became famous for its fashionable dressmakers – Madame Lucille used to be at No. 17 – and today the square is lined with a depressing hotch-potch of architecture, the latest specimens of modern office building cheek by jowl with heavyweights dating from the last century and a few experiments in *Art Nouveau*. But its graceful shape remains – each side is symmetrical and its tributary streets are harmoniously placed in relation to the whole. It is a few years earlier than Grosvenor Square, and a third of its size. Like Berkeley Square, it is built on a slope.

Oxford Street or the Tyburn Road to the north led to the gallows where Marble Arch stands now, and the noisy processions which followed the condemned man sitting in a cart with his coffin beside him often disturbed the elegant calm of the aristocratic square, but aroused little pity. Our 18th-century ancestors saw nothing morally wrong in the spectacle of a thief or a highwayman or even a young mother with a child at her breast having the life choked out of them – the quality as well as the riff-raff wallowed in London's largest free spectacle offered at the invitation of the State. The executions at Tyburn attended with 'so great mobbing and impertinencies' held up property development of this part of London as the fashionable world moved westward. (In 1726, the year King George's gilded statue was put up in Grosvenor Square, a woman was burned at the stake.) That is why the gallows were removed to Newgate in 1783. In Rocque's map there is a bald empty space where the gallows stood and Oxford Street was never fashionable because of the upheaval caused by the processions on execution day, Monday.

Thomas Pennant, the London historian, who was born in 1726, remembered Oxford Street as a deep hollow road, and full of sloughs – the lurking place of cut-throats. Fashion turned its back on the road leading to the Triple Tree. Do the shopping crowds that swarm down modern Oxford Street ever pause to think of the sad and terrible past of this *Via Dolorosa* along which some 50,000 at a rough estimate – peers and paupers, priests, coiners, murderers, boys who had stolen a few pence, clergymen and forgers – proceeded to their doom over a period of 500 years?

Harewood Place on the north side of Hanover Square leading into Oxford Street takes its name from Harewood House, built by Robert Adam for the Duke of Roxburghe, the famous book collector, and bought by the Earl of Harewood in 1804. It was a long three-storey house with a *porte-cochère* and a bow projecting into Harewood Place and its front in Hanover Square. The public hangings at Tyburn had been discontinued by the time the Duke of Roxburghe built here, otherwise he would not have chosen such an exposed site. Nevertheless, a row of posts shut off his house from the common thoroughfare, making it clear

13. 44, GROSVENOR SQUARE. No. 44, Grosvenor Square and its neighbour No. 43 date from the earliest days of the square and have survived in almost their original state. No. 44, the home of Lady Illingworth, is the last private house in the square. (Swaebe)

14. GARDEN IN GROSVENOR SQUARE. Lady Illingworth watering the flowers in her garden at the back of her house, No. 44, Grosvenor Square. (Swaebe)

15. GROSVENOR SQUARE MURALS. The murals discovered behind the panelling in the upstairs drawing room of No. 44, Grosvenor Square are thought to be by William Kent. They once formed part of the decoration over the staircase.

16. GROSVENOR STREET. Sir Richard Grosvenor planned Grosvenor Street as a long vista leading to the classical front of St George's Hanover Square. But buildings were allowed to bulge forward at the end of the street and in Maddox Street, masking the church except for the tip of its spire.

to outsiders that this was an exclusive part of London where the mob was not expected to be seen. Later they were replaced by gates which were closed to carriage traffic. Several of these barriers were erected in Mayfair. A row of posts shut off Burlington Gardens from Vigo Street, and there was a gate between Hanover Square and Brook Street and another barrier at the side of St George's Church in Maddox Street, emphasising the private character of Mayfair.

The pair of iron gates which shut off Harewood Place from Oxford Street were open only when Lord Harewood was in residence, and they remained *in situ* for a remarkably long time, not disappearing until 1894 by which time they had become an anachronism. When they were finally removed it was found that a family by the name of Fallen, having kept a fruit stall in front of them for several generations, had acquired squatting rights. They could not stay where they were in the middle of Harewood Place, but they were allowed to carry on business at the side of the street, though there is no trace today of them or anyone else in the soft fruit trade, not even a barrow boy, who would be quickly moved on by the police in this notorious bottle-neck.

William Pitt in bronze on his high pedestal turns his back to Hanover Square and looks down St George Street.[1] He is skied up on his perch as this was the wish – almost the condition – of the sculptor, Sir Francis Chantrey. The statue was put in place early one morning and when the workmen left for their breakfast having done their job, a party of reformers – it was the troubled political year of 1831 – threw a rope round Pitt's neck and tried to bring him down. But the statue stuck fast, and when Chantrey arrived on the scene for the unveiling ceremony he explained the reason – the cramps were 'leaded' and the reformers could have pulled until Domesday. Chantrey was an expensive sculptor. He charged £7,000 for Pitt. He not only claimed expenses but charged his clients for labour and materials as well, as we can see from his account book kept at Burlington House. No wonder that he died so rich, leaving the Royal Academy about £3,000 a year for buying works of art under the Chantrey Bequest. He started his career as a penniless student in an attic in Curzon Street, moving to Charles Street in the days of his affluence.

Hanover Square seems to have formed part of a general plan to co-ordinate the new buildings north and south of Oxford Street. Just as Sir Richard Grosvenor aligned Grosvenor Street to lead up towards the west façade of St George's – unsuccessfully as it turned out – so Hanover

[1] Formerly George Street.

Square was laid out with its southern side giving an oblique view down St George Street of the classical portico and steeple of the church, and was balanced on the north of Oxford Street by Cavendish Square.

The vista of St George's from Hanover Square won high praise from contemporary writers on London. Even that jaundiced observer, James Ralph, in his *Critical Review of the Public Buildings in and about London* of 1734 wrote:

> The view down George Street from the upper end of the Square is one of the most entertaining in this whole city; the sides of the square, the area in the middle, the break of the buildings that form the entrance to the vista, the vista itself, but above all the beautiful projection of the portico of St George's Church, are all circumstances that unite in beauty and render the scene perfect.

Some sixty years later another observer, T. A. Malton, in his *Picturesque Tour through the Cities of London and Westminster*, thought the view had 'more the air of an Italian scene than any other in London'. It also won praise from Wordsworth, who considered it one of the finest views in old London, and he was a connoisseur of London views.

Luckily this fine vista of the portico and soaring spire of St George's still remains, though the old Georgian houses lining St George Street are fast disappearing, and we can enjoy the same view of the church which a trotting chairman or gorgeously arrayed coachman on his box saw two hundred and fifty years ago.

CHAPTER FOUR

Churches and Chapels

THE FAMOUS and the fashionable have come to St George's, Hanover Square, Mayfair's parish church, to be married. A hundred years ago the *bon ton* decreed that a fashionable wedding could take place in no other church, and Victorian maidens by the score after a season of balls, routs and evenings at the opera, began their married life at its altar rails like the bride in Locker Lampson's poem, *St George's*, who

> *. . . passed up the aisle on the arm of her sire*
> *A delicate lady in bridal attire*
> *Fair emblem of virgin simplicity.*
> *Half London was there, and my word! there were few*
> *Who stood by the altar, or hid in a pew*
> *But envied Lord Nigel's felicity.*

On the occasion of a fashionable wedding the narrow streets near the church were crammed with carriages, while the elegantly dressed members of London society stood shoulder to shoulder in the pews and overflowed into the galleries. Afterwards the congregation would repair to the home of the bride's parents for the sumptuous wedding breakfast, the wedding cake supplied by Gunter's of Berkeley Square without which no marriage in high-life was complete.

It is often stated – especially in guide books – that Lady Hamilton was married at St George's. 'Dearest Emma' was a familiar figure in Mayfair, flitting between Bond Street and Grosvenor Square on Nelson's remaining arm, but she never entered St George's as a bride. As Emmy Lyon she was married to Sir William Hamilton at St Marylebone Parish Church, which had long associations with the Hamilton family, on September 6th, 1791. The confusion with St George's may have arisen because she

63

acted as witness to a wedding there on one occasion, signing the register as Emma Hamilton, on January 12th, 1797.

Among the many famous names entered in St George's register in the following century the best known is the Duke of Wellington's, whose bold signature occurs again and again. He was always ready to give away a pretty Mayfair bride and was witness to his eldest son's marriage in 1839.

Benjamin Disraeli started his long residence in Mayfair when he left St George's with his rich bride on his arm, the widow of his friend and colleague in the House of Commons, Wyndham Lewis. For the next twenty years Mary Anne made a comfortable home for her young husband – he was ten years her junior – at Grosvenor Gate in Park Lane, the white house with the green shutters overlooking the Park which still stands. The newly wedded Mrs Disraeli had a very practical turn of mind and she noted down in her account book:

> Gloves 2/6d. In hand £300. Married 28.8.1839
> Dear Dizzy became my husband.

Ten years later St George's was the centre of tremendous excitement. The notorious 'Spanish' dancer, Lola Montez, had arrived in the capital post-haste from Munich, where she had been responsible for toppling King Ludwig off his throne, leaving the country on the verge of a revolution. She was not Spanish at all, but the daughter of Irish parents and was born in Limerick. However, Ludwig had fallen for her 'Spanish' charms, and she had been chased out of Bavaria. In London she settled in Mayfair, taking rooms in Half Moon Street, and accepted the first rich suitor to propose to her – a puppy of a Life Guard with £10,000 a year, and they were married at St George's with a flock of reporters besieging the church. The bride signed the registry as Maria de las Dolores de Landsfeld, as she had been made Comtesse de Landsfeld by love-sick Ludwig, and gave her father's name as 'Juan Parris, Colonel in the army' and described herself as a widow. Unfortunately her first husband proved to be alive, but before she could be accused of bigamy her young 'husband', George Heald, met his death by drowning, not that the marriage would have lasted long in any case.

Among all the fuss and flurry of fashionable young marriages at St George's there was one wedding which stands out since the bride was neither fashionable nor young. She was the great Victorian novelist, George Eliot who married the American banker, John Walter Cross on May 6th, 1880. It would certainly have looked odd if she had signed the

17. GROSVENOR SQUARE, WEST SIDE. All the houses on the west side of Grosvenor Square were demolished to make way for the functional United States Embassy. *See* Plate 18 below.

19. ST GEORGE'S PARISH. St George's Parish was carved out of St Martin-in-the-Fields and included present-day Mayfair, Belgravia and Pimlico. In the 18th century only Mayfair was populated. (Westminster Public Library)

register with that name, as 'George Eliot' was only a pseudonym; in fact, she signed with her maiden name, Mary Ann Evans. Aged 61, she was one of the more mature brides to enter London's most fashionable wedding church.

St George's marriage registry contains another American signature. Theodore ('Teddy') Roosevelt was married here to Edith Carow, on December 2nd, 1886, though the marriage went unnoticed at the time, as the 28-year-old future President of the United States could only claim to be the unsuccessful candidate for the Mayoralty of New York and the writer of a few books – a history of the Naval War of 1812, and some papers on ranch life from his experiences of living with the cowboys in the 'Bad Lands'. He entered his 'Rank or Profession' in the marriage certificate, not as politician, but simply 'Ranchman'. It was a quiet wedding, as he was a widower and he had no friends in England. He was staying at Brown's Hotel in Dover Street, and his bride at Buckland's in Brook Street – so it was a Mayfair wedding from every point of view. He solved the problem of finding a best man by inviting a new friend he had made on the boat coming over, the future Sir Cecil Spring-Rice, then starting his career at the Foreign Office. 'He had me married in bright orange gloves', Teddy Roosevelt recalled afterwards, 'which I accepted with a calm wholly unwarranted', though Sir Cecil Spring-Rice was far from being a dandy himself. His friendship with Roosevelt had a great influence on his career, for soon afterwards he applied for a posting as Secretary of Legation at Washington and years later returned there as British Ambassador and carried on the delicate negotiations during the first World War which led to the United States entering on the allied side.

A *Marriage à la Mode* at St George's which caught the public imagination in the 'nineties was the wedding between London's most talked-of young woman, Miss Margot Tennant, whose parents lived in Grosvenor Square, and the 42-year-old Home Secretary in Lord Rosebery's Liberal Government, Mr Herbert Asquith, on May 10th, 1894.

Lady Oxford has described in her memoirs the excitement that her wedding caused. Although it was raining, the streets all the way from her parents' home to St George's 'were blocked with excited and enthusiastic people', and there was a tremendous crowd trying to enter the church, the invited and the not-invited. Among the latter was a 'gentleman with a gardenia in his buttonhole', as Margot's old nurse described him, adding that she knew he was a gentlemen because he wore a gardenia.

He insisted 'on seeing Miss Tennant married', and offered her ten pounds for her ticket. But the old nannie would not part.

The wedding made history, as four Prime Ministers, past, present and to come, signed the register: Mr Gladstone (who gave the couple the seven volumes of his *Gleanings* as a wedding present), Lord Rosebery, Mr Balfour, and the bridegroom, who became Prime Minister in 1908. Mr Campbell-Bannerman, another future Prime Minister, was in the congregation, too. Among the ten bridesmaids dressed in white and carrying roses was the widower-bridegroom's little daughter, who grew up to be Lady Violet Bonham-Carter, now Baroness Asquith.

St George's reigned supreme as 'Hymen's classic Temple' until the end of the century, when its place was taken by St Paul's, Knightsbridge. Weddings were beginning to be more complicated. The bride's wedding dress was becoming an item of interest to the reading public and newspapers needed copy. So the 'wedding rehearsal' was introduced. St George's frowned on this worldly development, but St Paul's, Knightsbridge, took a more modern view, and allowed rehearsals to be held, which gave it a great advantage for holding society weddings.

St George's owes its origin to Queen Anne's High Church piety. The same elevating sentiments which abolished – temporarily – the Fair gave Mayfair its parish church. Two years after the Magistrates put an end to the riotous assembly on Brookfield, Parliament passed an Act very near to the Queen's heart, 'for the erection of 50 new churches in and about the cities of London and Westminster' to be paid for out of a tax on coal. Such an immense building programme – to provide the new residential districts like Mayfair with places of worship – was far too ambitious to be carried out in its entirety. Only a small number of the new churches were built, but St George's was one of them, with good reason, for by the time it was consecrated in 1725 a new town had grown up on the fields north of Piccadilly and the greatest in the land lived there. As long ago as 1689 Dr Tenison, Vicar of St Martin-in-the-Fields and later Archbishop of Canterbury – 'That public minded, charitable and pious man', Evelyn called him – foreseeing developments, erected a wooden chapel on Conduit Mead given him by King William. It had originally been a 'Popish' chapel used by King James II for hearing Mass when reviewing his troops on Hounslow Heath, and was on wheels. This is the small church with the sharply pointed steeple we see in the fields to the west of Burlington House garden in the Knyff-Kip engraving. Dr Tenison rededicated it to the Holy Trinity, and announced on July

19th, 1691, at the end of his sermon that the church 'should be made a Parish Church as soone as the Parliament sate', according to John Evelyn who was present. He worshipped there whenever in London, and his grand-daughter Jane was christened in the chapel. But Dr Tenison was disappointed and it was not until over a quarter of a century later that Mayfair had its parish church.

General William Steward, Queen Anne's Commander-in-Chief in Ireland, a rich parishioner, who was one of the first residents of Hanover Square, gave the land for the church and laid the foundation stone on June 20th, 1721, pouring out a libation of wine and pronouncing the words: 'Lord God of Heaven preserve the Church of St George.' The new parish carved out of that of St Martin-in-the-Fields covered the whole of what is now Mayfair, Belgravia and Pimlico. The architect was John James, a pupil of James Gibbs who built St Martin-in-the-Fields and St Mary Le Strand. Because of the bulge in Maddox Street our view of St George's from the front is lost and it is so hemmed in by buildings that it can only be seen either up or down St George Street. This may well be the reason why the statue of King George I, in whose honour the church was named, was never placed on the pediment over the portico as it would have been invisible except from the first floor windows of the houses opposite. The empty pedestal is still there.

The two black pointers sitting on their haunches under the portico were the gift to the church from a sporting tailor in Conduit Street, and they used to keep watch on the pavement outside his shop until it was bombed in the last war. He had no home for them, and St George's took them in.

Inside, the church walls are almost bare of tablets and memorials, as it was not used for burials. It has a vault, but it was let out to store wine until the Bishop of London objected, and now is used for storing books.

When St George's was built, there was no space for a graveyard in the precincts so the parish burial ground was laid out farther to the west between Mount Street and South Street; this soon filled up and another burial ground had to be opened north of Hyde Park in the Uxbridge Road near Tyburn. The Rectory used to be until 1937 at 15, Grosvenor Street. The Georgian house still stands, next to Mrs Keppel's old home.

St George's was renowned for the excellence of its preachers. A good preacher was essential financially, as the church's income depended largely on pew rents, and a popular preacher could fill a church. His portrait was sold in the print shops (in Victorian days it was his photograph) and he could count on a good sale for his sermons in volume form, though they make very tedious reading today. Laurence Sterne made £300 from a volume of his sermons. The average salary for a morning preacher was £50 and for an evening preacher £65. A good organist was another attraction, and St George's employed as its first organist Dr Roseingrave, the best in England – at £50 a year – who ended in a lunatic asylum.

Going to church was an important social occasion, and almost the same members of the elegant world of Mayfair attended divine service at St George's as a rout at Devonshire House. No church in England could boast such an aristocratic congregation. Resident in the parish in 1725 there were nine Dukes, two Marquesses, twenty-two Earls, six Viscounts, twelve Barons; also one Archbishop and two Bishops. The Vestry – to quote a guide book of 1732 – was composed 'of the chief nobility of England', as we can see from the titled names of the church wardens inscribed on the panels of the gallery. It is true that King George I was a churchwarden of St Martin-in-the-Fields, but the ornaments of his court were the churchwardens of St George's.

Preferment to the living – said to be worth £1,500 a year – could be very tempting to an 18th-century divine. It proved fatal to the unfortunate Dr William Dodd, a society parson with a great gift of oratory, a facile pen and a love of the good things of life. His many gifts won him a royal chaplaincy, but he aspired higher still – to be Rector of St George's in Mayfair. He caused a letter to be written – it is thought by his wife – to Lady Apsley, the wife of the Lord Chancellor, offering her a *douceur* of £3,000 and an annuity of £500 if she would recommend him to the living. The affair became public, and the scandal it caused started Dr Dodd on the downward path. Struck off the list of royal chaplains, he had to sell his share of the Charlotte Chapel in Pimlico of which he was part proprietor, and he 'even descended so low as to become the editor of a newspaper'. He incurred debts, and in desperation forged the signature of his patron, Lord Chesterfield, on a bond for £4,250. Forging a document was a capital offence, and the luckless parson was condemned to death.

His trial aroused national interest. Dr Johnson took up his cause and tried to intervene with the King, and thousands of signatures were collected. But Dr Dodd had to pay the supreme penalty. By an ironic stroke of fate his last journey from Newgate to Tyburn passed along the Oxford Road within sight of St George's, the Rectorship of which he had so fatally coveted. He was hanged at Tyburn on June 27th, 1777, his last moments watched by the largest crowd ever known there, the gaping spectators perched on trees, filling the huge grandstands erected for the occasion, known as 'Mother Proctor's pews', and packing the rooftops.

Elias Martin, the Swedish artist who was living 'at Miss Laverrock's, Milliner' in Mill Street, painted the oblique view of St George's – so popular with artists – from Hanover Square. In his picture, exhibited at the Royal Academy in 1770, the plain looking building with the gabled roof in Conduit Street where the Westbury Hotel now stands is Trinity Chapel. This was the successor to the wooden chapel which Dr Tenison dedicated, hoping it would become the new parish church, but as the land was held on lease the Church authorities opposed the plan. Instead it was rebuilt in brick in 1716, and became a proprietary chapel, remaining in the parish of St Martin-in-the-Fields even after St George's parish was formed around it.

Mayfair had several of these proprietary chapels, which were built as an investment by private persons, who saw that there was money to be made in fashionable piety. They were not usually consecrated and Holy Communion could be celebrated only with a licence from the Bishop. A captivating preacher was essential if the chapel was to pay as he drew the crowds who rented the pews. He mounted the pulpit in scented lawn holding a bouquet, and with a diamond ring glittering on his finger preached before a congregation of fair penitents who prayed in patches, sued for pardon in paint and saw their heaven in man. Thackeray called these snug chapels 'preaching boxes', and a Bishop of London dismissed them laconically as 'all venal and all ten percenters'.

Trinity Chapel was bought by a bookseller in New Bond Street, James Robson, who fitted up the inside with 'great neatness and propriety', rebuilt the front and – most important – engaged the popular preacher, Dr Beamish, who soon attracted the fashionable world to his chapel. He drew such crowds that extra galleries had to be installed. When Robson's 99-year lease expired, the chapel was pulled down and the valuable site sold in 1877 and shops erected in its place.

The most notorious of the Mayfair chapels was the Mayfair Chapel itself – sometimes known as the Curzon Chapel – which was run on strict business lines by Dr Alexander Keith, a marriage broker in holy orders. Built about 1730 in the heart of old May Fair, it was a plain red brick chapel with a cupola facing Crewe House in Curzon Street.

'Fleet Marriages', which at the time were legal though irregular, were performed there without licence, certificate of banns or consent of parents. Couples could be married straight from the street. 'Happy's the wooing that's not a long a-doing' was this irreverent gentleman's motto.

Appointed incumbent of the Mayfair Chapel in 1734, Dr Keith took advantage of his splendid opportunities and charged one guinea for each marriage. Soon he was marrying couples at a furious rate, making a very bishopric of a revenue, in the words of Horace Walpole, out of the marriage fees, which went straight into his own pocket, although the chapel was in the parish of St George's. He became widely known through his advertisements in the Press, and in 1742 he solemnised seven hundred marriages – worth seven hundred guineas – compared with a mere forty at St George's, Hanover Square.

It was his last good year, because the rector of St George's, Dr Trebeck, took steps to put an end to the scandal and excommunicated his parson. What did Dr Keith do then? Ever resourceful, he counter-attacked with the same weapon, and excommunicated not only Dr Trebeck, but the Bishop of the Diocese and the Judge. To no avail, because in April of the following year he was committed to the Fleet Prison. Nevertheless marriages at a guinea a time still continued to be celebrated in the Mayfair Chapel by his assistants until they were turned out, when they moved to a house on the opposite side of the street, the 'firm' still trading under the same name as the advertisement in the *London Gazette* of January 12th, 1749, makes clear:

> The way to Dr Keith's Chapel is through Piccadilly by the End of St James's Street, and down Clarges Street, and turn on the Left-hand. The Marriages (together with a Licence on a Five Shilling Stamp and Certificate) are carried on for a Guinea, as usual, and Time till Four in the Afternoon, by another regular Clergyman, at Dr Keith's Little Chapel in May Fair, near Hyde Park Corner, opposite the great Chapel, and within ten yards of it. There is a Porch at the Door like a Country Church Porch.

It was astute to provide the Little Chapel with a porch, as this was an age which still remembered that it was in a porch that weddings used to be solemnised. The advertisement was so worded to give the impression that Dr Keith was still in charge. He was an adept at publicity, and even used his wife's corpse as an advertisement. She died while he was in the

Fleet, whereupon he had her body embalmed and put on show, and the *Daily Advertiser* wrote on January 23rd, 1750:

> We are informed that Mrs Keith's corpse was removed from her husband's house in May Fair in the middle of October to an apothecary in South Audley Street where she lies in a room hung with mourning and is to continue there until Dr Keith can attend the funeral . . .

Then follows an advertisement like the one above giving information about the guinea marriages and details about how to find the Little Chapel.

Among the marriages performed at the Little Chapel was that of the Duke of Hamilton with the beautiful Elizabeth Gunning, amusingly chronicled – as so many other happenings in Mayfair at this date – by Horace Walpole, Mayfair's chief gossip, who wrote to Sir Horace Mann on February 27th, 1752, that the Duke made love to Miss Gunning at an assembly given by Lord Chesterfield at his new house and, two nights later,

> being left alone with her while her mother and sister were at Bedford House, he found himself so impatient that he sent for a parson. The Doctor refused to perform the ceremony without licence and ring. The Duke swore he would send for the Archbishop; at last they were married with a ring of the bed curtain, at half past twelve at night at May Fair Chapel.

The Marriage Act of 1753 finally put an end to the lucrative business carried on at the Little Chapel, but right up to the end Dr Keith's assistants were marrying couples for all they were worth, and on the day before Lady Day, 1754, when Lord Hardwicke's Act came into force, sixty-one marriages were performed, so if the chapel opened its doors at seven o'clock an average of about six marriages must have been performed in an hour, or one every ten minutes. In all about seven thousand of these marriages were performed by Dr Keith and his assistant clerics, bringing in some seven thousand guineas. Nevertheless, Dr Keith died in poverty in Fleet Prison in 1758. He was also an author, writing the edifying book *The Guide, or The Christian Pathway to Everlasting Life*.

Dr Keith's Chapel and its record of irregular marriages added an extra attraction to the May Fair, and many an innocent maiden straying into the Fair found a husband sooner than she had dreamed with such opportunities at hand for a quick marriage and no questions asked. The popular

ditty, *The Lady's Ramble to May Fair*, very likely ended at the busy altar of the Little Chapel:

> '*From grave lessons and restraint*
> *I'm stole out to revel here,*
> *Yet I tremble and I pant*
> *In the middle of the Fair*
> *Oh, oh, oh would fortune in my way,*
> *Throw a lover kind and gay.*
> *Now's ye time, now's ye time*
> *He may soon move a heart unus'd to love.*
> *Shall I venture?*
> *No. No. No.*
> *Shall I from ye danger go?*
> *No. No. No.*
> *I must not try*
> *I cannot fly*
> *I must not, durst not, cannot fly.*
> *I must not try*
> *I cannot fly*
> *I must not, durst not, cannot fly.*'

The song must have enjoyed great popularity in 1739, the year it was published, and we can hear it being bawled out in the smoky tap rooms of the Three Jolly Butchers and the Dog and Duck.

The Mayfair Chapel was pulled down in November, 1899,[1] and the site sold for £26,000 to make way for the last great mansion to be built in Mayfair, Sunderland House, which was a wedding present from old Commodore Vanderbilt to his daughter Consuelo on her marriage to the Duke of Marlborough. Madame Balsan, as she became later, tells us in her memoirs that they were hard put to give their new house a name. The obvious choice was Marlborough House, but there could not be a second Marlborough House in London. The Prince of Wales, then living at Marlborough House in St James's, suggested they should call it Malplaquet House, a sly dig at the house's cramped position on the edge of Shepherd Market, which Madame Balsan herself refers to in her memoirs as a slum. Eventually they chose to name it after the Earldom of Sunderland, one of the Marlborough titles.

[1] The communion plate was presented to the parish church of Penn, Buckinghamshire, by the late Lord Howe in 1963.

The splendid house was built on hallowed ground, which is always considered unlucky. The vault had been used for storing wine, a common practice at the time, as Theodore Hook's lines recall:

> *The worshipper in this chapel should know*
> *There's a spirit above and a spirit below.*
> *The spirit above is the Spirit Divine*
> *But the Spirit below is the spirit of wine.*

The Duchess of Marlborough hoped that in removing the source of temptation by emptying the vault of the wine the spirit above would be placated. But to no avail. Sunderland House turned out be an unlucky house. Soon the marriage broke up, ending in divorce, and a bomb damaged it badly in an air raid during the last war. But it still stands, now called Lombard House, its French Renaissance architecture coming as a surprise in Curzon Street. It cost £350,000, one of the most expensive wedding presents ever given. Trebeck Street,[1] which runs down to the east side of Sunderland House into Shepherd Market, is named after Dr Trebeck, the first Rector of St George's, Hanover Square, who had the famous battle ecclesiastical with Dr Keith, whose notorious 'Little Chapel' stood just here on the left side of the street on entering from Curzon Street.

The greatest of all preachers, the Rev. Sydney Smith, Canon of St Paul's, made his reputation in Mayfair. He was engaged as Morning Preacher at the Berkeley Chapel, still another place of worship in Mayfair, and only a few steps away from the Curzon Chapel. It was also a proprietary chapel, built about 1750 by a member of the Berkeley family on Berkeley land, and stood at the corner of John Street, now Chesterfield Gardens, and Charles Street, and was a very handsome building with a cupola and a Doric porch.

Sydney Smith – the Smith of Smiths – thundered at his congregation and did not spare their feelings. Crowds flocked to hear him; at the same time he was lecturing on moral philosophy at the Royal Institution in Albemarle Street and preaching the evening sermon at the Fitzroy Chapel in Fitzroy Square. One day while in the full flight of his oratory at the Berkeley Chapel his torrent of words was interrupted by a loud 'Ahem . . . Ahem' from the back of the congregation. It came from Lord Dudley, an eccentric peer, notorious for his embarrassing habit of thinking aloud.

[1] Formerly East Chapel Street.

Dr Lee of Lambeth was incumbent at the Berkeley Chapel for a short period (1856–8) and his description of its comforts and aristocratic congregation is quoted by H. R. T. Brandreth in his *Dr Lee of Lambeth*:

> This building, the freehold of which was in possession of an Oxford man, Mr Francis Tate, Vicar of Axminster, who appointed me, was a fashionable place of worship as unsatisfactory as it could be. It was coloured inside and out by what London painters term 'a warm drab', and upholstered throughout with pink velvet and heavy hangings on brass rods. Its prominent ornament was a very handsome highly polished and useful stove which greatly dwarfed the undersized communion table. The chapel, however, had an aristrocratic and eminently select congregation – peers and peeresses, and their offspring. . . . There was a rich odour of human nature throughout the place and the congregation fanned itself or used smelling salts. The preacher's manners were those of a very superior person, and he appeared ever conscious of having been made so.

On cold days a cheerful fire crackled in the stove placed in the very centre of the aisle, which was carpeted with 'cozy Brussels' according to the Rev. C. M. Davies in *Orthodox London* who was struck by the 'downy' aspect of the place when T. Teignmouth Shore was incumbent. Matins started at the easy hour for Mayfair of 11.30 a.m. and the clergyman entered 'gorgeous in Oxford hood and tin-black stole preceded by a funny little gentleman in a green wig and scarf half a yard broad, who seemed to represent the genius of the chapel itself in its earliest times'.

The Duke of Clarence worshipped in the Berkeley Chapel and after his early death which so shocked the nation – he was engaged to Princess May, later Queen Mary – a stained glass window was erected to his memory there. It was unveiled by the Duchess of Teck, Princess May's mother, but what became of it when the chapel was demolished in 1907 is not known. It was probably broken up, as there is no trace of it either at Windsor Castle or Sandringham.

Only one of Mayfair's many chapels still survives, the Grosvenor Chapel in South Audley Street, where Sir Richard Grosvenor worshipped, occupying the front row of the gallery which was reserved for his family. A syndicate built it as a speculation – 'Benjamin Timbrell, carpenter, Robert Scott, carpenter, William Barlow, senior bricklayer, and Robert Andrews, gentleman', paying £20 p.a. ground rent; and it was run up cheaply by a builder in Mount Street. Sir Richard Grosvenor had his say in the siting of the chapel since it was on his estate, and it looks down the long vista of Aldford Street (formerly Chapel Street) to Hyde Park, its classical façade and sky blue spire coming as a delightful surprise when seen from Park Lane. It shows how effective St George's west front would have looked at the end of an even longer vista.

Sir Richard took a personal interest in the chapel and presented the magnificent organ to the proprietors, but it was only finished the year before he died in 1731. When its 99-year lease expired the parish bought it for £2,000 and the old proprietary chapel is now a chapel-of-ease belonging to St George's with a congregation drawn from all over London.

The chapel's plain exterior is matched by the austere white walls inside and the tall windows which flood it with light, but its 18th-century simplicity is unfortunately spoilt by Sir Ninian Comper's modern reredos. It abuts St George's burial ground, and also has a vault of its own where many famous Mayfair residents are buried. An air of mystery hangs over the vault, as no one has entered it for a hundred years, and the Priest-in-Charge has not been able to find the way down. Probings with steel rods have been made, holes dug, but with no result. It is known to contain the bodies of Lady Mary Wortley Montagu, John Wilkes (whose epitaph, 'A Friend of Liberty', which he wrote himself, is in the gallery), James Robson, the New Bond Street bookseller who owned Trinity Chapel, and the Earl and Countess of Mornington, the parents of the great Duke of Wellington. Lord Chesterfield left instructions that he should be buried in the graveyard nearest to where he died, and as he died at Chesterfield House he was brought here, but his body was removed later to Shelford in Nottinghamshire.

The probings started after the present Duke of Wellington inquired whether he could place a plaque in the church to the memory of his ancestors, the Earl and Countess of Mornington, and see their coffins, but no entrance could be found. There may be a clue in the date – 1859 – when permission was granted for the last burial in the vault. It was in January, 1859, that an Order in Council was published warning that remains, if so wished, had to be removed from the vault in St Martin-in-the-Fields before February 1st of the same year, after which the vault would be closed and 'could not be inspected under any pretence whatever'. Probably the vault of the Grosvenor Chapel was closed up for hygienic reasons at the same date. Francis Buckland tells us in his *Curiosities of Natural History* that reading the notice in *The Times* he hurried off to

St Martin's and obtained permission to extract the coffin of John Hunter, the celebrated physician, and arranged for his remains to be buried in Westminster Abbey. No one was sufficiently interested to extract the coffins of Lady Mary Wortley Montagu, John Wilkes or any others buried in the vault of the Chapel before it was closed up for ever. There they sleep their last sleep, a strange assembly – revolutionary and lady of letters, bookseller and earl and countess, and many others – only a few feet under South Audley Street, and they will not be disturbed until the sounding of the last trump.

A world-famous woman who spent her time in furious work in an upper room in her house in South Street, seeing no one yet in touch with everyone, belonged to the congregation of the Grosvenor Chapel: Florence Nightingale. Her house, No. 10,[1] South Street (now demolished) looked over the garden of Dorchester House, and she lived there for nearly half a century until her death in 1910. A letter she wrote to the recently arrived minister of the Grosvenor Chapel, the Rev. R. S. Oldham, is framed in the vestry. It deals with her favourite topic, requesting him when he became familiar with the neighbourhood:

> to bear us in mind and if you find any good young woman, whether gentlewoman or more especially a woman of the working class, sound and healthy in body and mind, who would like to be trained as a Hospital Nurse to address her to our Training Matron.

And she ends:

> I am troubling you too much, but you are our pastor. Under severe stress of business and illness

> > ever your faithful servant
> > Florence Nightingale.

She generously enclosed a gift of two guineas, and, as was her custom, added the exact time of writing the letter: September 5th, 1878. 6 a.m.

The Grosvenor Chapel drew the most fashionable congregation in London, according to W. J. Loftie, writing in the eighteen-eighties. Although there were so many churches and chapels in Mayfair each one was packed twice a day on Sundays. No one left town at the week-end and going to church offered a diversion to our Victorian ancestors, especially as in Mayfair it was followed by Church Parade in Hyde Park.

No account of Mayfair's churches would be complete without a

[1] No. 35, old numbering.

mention of Church Parade, the weekly ritual that took place every Sunday morning during the season after church on the strip of grass and gravel between Stanhope Gate and the Achilles statue. Here a highly fashionable, highly decorous crowd carrying their prayer books promenaded under the trees between church and luncheon. No crush, no excitement: merely a stately gliding to and fro and a murmuring of quiet voices, with the ripple of polite laughter as friends greeted each other. Silk hats and frock coats were *de rigueur* for men and the ladies paraded in their best. By some unwritten law no one took part who did not belong, yet there was a complete lack of formality. Thousands paraded up and down the strip of grass – nearly all churchgoers, it must be said – and after the short parade was over and it was time to repair to a heavy Sunday luncheon, one top-hatted habitué might be heard to remark to another as he waved his gloved hand in farewell: 'Quite a good Park today.'

Church Parade never recovered from the first World War, though a few of the older generation tried to carry on the tradition in the nineteen-twenties. It died a natural death, partly because of the growing habit of spending the week-end out of London, and partly because of the slump.

During the last war the Grosvenor Chapel was used by the American armed forces who gave thanks for the allied victory here as a plaque on the front recalls. Its simple classical lines and plain glass windows, which flood the chalk white interior with light, must have reminded many of the Americans of their old churches at home, as the Grosvenor Chapel was taken as a model for colonial churches.

Mayfair has one Roman Catholic church, the well-known Church of the Jesuit Fathers in Farm Street, which dates from 1844, an important date in the history of St George's parish as this was the year when its boundaries were redrawn. By then Mayfair's remaining building plots were few, and the new church had to be fitted in as best possible and was built in a stable lane known as Berkeley Mews; it faces north-west instead of east. Cardinal Manning was received into the Roman Catholic Church here on Passion Sunday, 1851, and he said his first Mass at Farm Street. It became a parish church in 1965.

Another church in a cramped position is Christ Church, Down Street, built in 1865 on land belonging to the Dean and Chapter of Westminster with its main entrance close to the High Altar. Like the Farm Street church it is built in neo-Gothic, a rare style of architecture in Mayfair. Its parish, carved out of St George's, included Shepherd Market and reached as far east as Stratton Street. Devonshire House was on its borders and it was at Christ Church, Down Street, that the Duke of Devonshire made the Duchess of Manchester into the 'Double Duchess' in 1892.

The parish of St Mark's, North Audley Street, which extends along the northern section of Mayfair between Park Street and Regent Street, was also carved out of St George's. The church might almost be missed at first as its neo-classical front is built flush with the terrace of houses on the east side of the street. It is the work of J. P. Gandy-Deering, a Regency architect whose style was influenced by a visit to Greece, but only the classical façade of his original church remains. Sir Arthur Blomfield, son of Charles James Blomfield, Bishop of London, the architect of so many churches, remodelled its interior in an ornate Byzantine style with Norman undertones. Immediately inside the main entrance on the right is the monument to Sir Hudson Lowe, Governor of St Helena and Napoleon's gaoler, who is buried in the crypt with his wife. He died a disappointed and embittered man aged 77, having spent the years since his retirement trying to vindicate his name from the calumnies cast on him by O'Meara in his record *The Voice of St Helena*.

St Mark's was originally a chapel-of-ease in the Parish of St George's and mainly intended for the tenements south of Oxford Street. It became fashionable after it was rebuilt and the rows of pews still bear the small gilt frames for holding the visiting cards of the pew renters, but they are nearly all without cards now. The church seats 1350.

Church building in Mayfair slowed down as the century ended, and the King's Weigh House Chapel, in Duke Street off Grosvenor Square, dating from 1891, was one of the last, but its origins go back to the 17th century, as the first church of that name stood in Cornhill and was burned down in the Great Fire. It is a Congregational church designed by Waterhouse in harsh brick and terracotta with a spire: an ugly building. The United States Navy uses it as its chapel.

The last church to be built in Mayfair is the Third Church of Christ Scientist of 1912. Its tower looking down Half Moon Street is a well-known Piccadilly landmark standing next to the Washington Hotel.

Among Mayfair's vanished churches mention should be made of St George's Chapel, Albemarle Street, built in 1815. Fashionable church going was carried here to such an extreme that a service was held at nine o'clock on Sunday evening to allow the congregation to have dinner first, and they came on afterwards usually in full evening dress, the men in white tie and tail coats and the ladies in long evening gowns, wearing their jewels as if they were attending a gala night at Covent Garden.

Pews at the Albemarle Street chapel were a marketable commodity as this advertisement in *The Times* of May 8th, 1846, shows:

> ST GEORGE'S CHAPEL, Albemarle-Street – To be SOLD, for 40 guineas, about 65 years of the unexpired LEASE of a PEW for five persons, situate near the communion table. Inquire of Mr Wild, fruiterer and greengrocer, Curzon-Street, Mayfair.

The chapel, which stood at the top end of Albemarle Street on the west, was closed in 1904 and its contents auctioned. A crowd of dealers crowded into the chapel jostling the fashionable people who had come for the sake of old associations. The chief lot was the organ whose notes had accompanied the voices of such well known singers as Madame Nordica, Madame Bella Cole and Dame Clara Butt. It was knocked down for 360 guineas and was bought for the Church of St Barnabas at Hove.

St Saviour's, Oxford Street, for the Deaf and Dumb, designed by Sir Arthur Blomfield, also is no more. It was built on ground given by the Duke of Westminster, and the Prince of Wales laid the foundation stone in 1870. The Duke showed great interest in church building on his estate. He owned a private chapel in Park Street, St Mary's, an 18th-century building with portico and cupola, and when this was demolished in 1882 he built St Mary's in Bourdon Street, quite close to Bourdon House, to replace it, laying the foundation stone himself. This was also designed by Blomfield and is one of his best works in London. The Rev. Dick Shepherd, who later became the popular Vicar of St Martin's, was in charge from 1911–1913, and filled it to the doors. It was closed before the second World War and used as a store. In 1940 when the Dutch community in London lost their church in Austin Friars in the City they were given hospitality here, as a plaque made of blue and white Dutch tiles, the gift of the Protestant Churches in the Netherlands (now in the porch of St George's Hanover Square) recalls: 'I was a stranger and ye took me in'. St Mary's was demolished in 1961 and the site after being used as a car park is now an office block.

The Hanover Chapel in Regent Street is another of the vanished churches of Mayfair: it belonged to the parish of St George's and seated a thousand. It was built by C. R. Cockerell in 1823 as part of Nash's great plan for Regent Street and with its squat towers and Greek Ionic portico projecting into the street was a familiar London landmark. In spite of protests it was demolished by Act of Parliament in 1897 and the

20. ST GEORGE'S, HAN-
OVER SQUARE. The oblique
view of St George's seen
from the north side of
Hanover Square painted by
the Swedish artist, Elias
Martin. The chapel in the
far distance is Trinity
Chapel in Conduit Street.
(National Museum, Stock-
holm)

21. TRINITY CHAPEL.
Trinity Chapel, Conduit
Street, as rebuilt by James
Robson, the New Bond
Street bookseller, in 1777.
(London Museum)

22. **Mayfair Chapel.**
Curzon Street in the
nineties with Dr
Keith's Mayfair
Chapel on the right.
(National Monuments
Record)

23. **Mayfair Marriage 'Licence'.** Dr
Alexander Keith married without licence,
banns or consent of
parents. Couples on
leaving his Mayfair
Chapel received a
document signed by
him giving his consent to their marriage.
(Collection of Mr
Gordon Barnes)

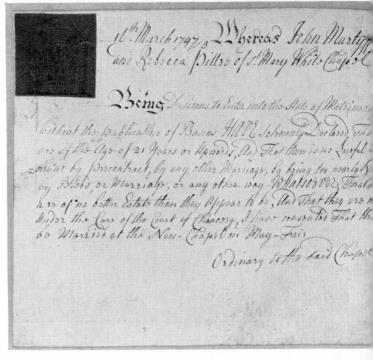

24. A *Vanity Fair* cartoon of the Duke of Cambridge driving his phaeton in Mayfair.

25. BERKELEY CHAPEL. The Duke of Clarence worshipped at the Berkeley Chapel and after his early death a memorial window was placed in the Chapel, which was unveiled by the Duchess of Teck, the mother of his intended bride, Princess Mary, later Queen Mary. (Westminster Public Library)

26. **GLOUCESTER HOUSE, PARK LANE.** Gloucester House at the corner of Piccadilly and Park Lane was a royal residence for nearly a century.

27. **CHAOS IN PARK LANE.** Horse buses, private carriages, herds of cattle, donkey carts and terrified pedestrians wedged in the narrow gulley of Old Park Lane in the 1860s.

site sold for £43,000. An inscription on Regent House, between Hanover Street and Princes Street, recalls that the Hanover Chapel once stood there.

The demolition of the Hanover Chapel must have weighed heavily on the conscience of the Crown Commissioners who owned the site, as they set apart nearly half the money for the building of a replacement – St Anselm's in Davies Street. The foundation stone was laid by the Duke and Duchess of Westminster, and it was opened in 1898. Designed in early Renaissance style, it was acknowledged as one of the outstanding examples of church building of the last quarter of the 19th century. Thackeray Turner was the architect, a pupil of Sir Gilbert Scott, and the secretary of the Society for the Protection of Ancient Buildings. But the decline of church going had already set in, and it was demolished in 1938. The British Council block stands on the site, and only St Anselm's Place reminds us that a church once stood there.

The draining away of Mayfair's population has meant that congregations in the few remaining churches are small. Mayfair has suffered the same fate as the City. The list of streets in St George's parish are posted up in the church porch, and they are nearly all shopping streets. How many residents has Hanover Square today or Old Bond Street, built by Sir Thomas Bond for the 'nobility and gentry'? Very few. The change is reflected in the number of marriages celebrated in Mayfair's parish church. The figure averages under 35 a year now at St George's, compared with ten and twelve a day at the beginning of the last century when the annual total was between 1,100 and 1,200.

CHAPTER FIVE

Royal Mayfair

MAYFAIR, UNLIKE KENSINGTON, has no royal palace within its boundaries, and it has never been the home of a reigning sovereign except for the short period after the abdication of King Edward VIII when King George VI continued to live at his town house, 145, Piccadilly, the first time a King of England had ever lived in a street. It was his home as Duke of York before he moved to Buckingham Palace.

Our present Queen spent much of her childhood at this house, one of the large Victorian mansions standing next to Apsley House, with a garden at the back; and one of the memories of the 1930s is the glimpse from the top of a bus rounding Hyde Park Corner of Princess Elizabeth and Princess Margaret playing with their corgies on the lawn. The house was badly bombed during the war, and has vanished like the house where the Queen was born in Bruton Street.

Mayfair grew up under the first Georges. It was the new part of town, the 'court end' with St James's Palace down the hill to the south and Kensington Palace beyond Hyde Park to the west. Landlords and owners of property went out of their way to pay compliments to the reigning sovereign and the House of Hanover. St George's Church and George Street were named in honour of the King, and Hanover Square in honour of his House. If Sir Richard Grosvenor's plan had been carried out, King George I's statue would have looked down Grosvenor Street to the Park from its vantage point over the portico of St George's as a counterpart to the equestrian statue in Grosvenor Square. Berkeley Square, too, had its royal statue – of King George III on his horse under the trees. The custom of honouring the House of Hanover in Mayfair is still very much alive as one can see from the number of entries in the London Telephone

Directory with the word 'Hanover' in their title: Hanover Car Hire, Hanover Gallery, Hanover Hairdressing, Hanover Press . . .

Whether the Georges appreciated the compliments from their contemporaries is not recorded. Instances of the monarch visiting the house of a subject in London are extremely rare in the 18th century, and neither of the first two Hanoverian kings seems to have singled out any Mayfair resident for this honour, unlike King William III who dined with the Duke of Devonshire soon after he took up residence at Berkeley House. For many years the only 'royal' resident in Mayfair after Princess Anne was King George's mistress, the 'Maypole' – not a very desirable personage whose name stank in the nostrils of most Englishmen.

From the reign of King George III onwards royal links with Mayfair grow stronger. The King himself and Queen Charlotte who had musical tastes often drove to Hanover Square, to attend the Hanover Square Concert and Ball Room where J. C. Bach, son of Sebastian Bach, performed on the harpsichord with consummate art.

The King's brother, the Duke of Gloucester, lived in Mayfair, at Gloucester House on the edge of Hyde Park where Tyburn Lane skirted the Park wall, the site of Grosvenor House today. The Duke had a quarrel with the King over his morganatic marriage with a beautiful widow, Maria Dowager Countess Waldegrave, whom he married without the King's knowledge or consent. To make her still less acceptable, Lady Waldegrave was illegitimate, as her father, Sir Edward Walpole, had never bothered to marry her mother, Dorothy Clement, the daughter of the postmaster at Darlington, and she also brought three orphaned daughters with her. The Duke did not live with his wife at Gloucester House, and their marriage remained secret for six years, as he did not reveal it to the King until it became known that his brother, the Duke of Cumberland, had married morganatically too.

The Duke had fallen in love with a pretty widow, Mrs Anne Horton, and married her in that lady's drawing room in Hertford Street not a stone's throw from Dr Keith's notorious Mayfair Chapel. The marriages of both royal Dukes were legal, but the King, who cut off all communications with his brothers, was determined that no such unions should be made in future and the Royal Marriage Act was passed in 1772, by which no marriage of a member of the royal family was legal without the consent of the Sovereign.

To little effect, however, as two of the King's sons married in defiance of the Act – George, Prince of Wales with Mrs Fitzherbert, and Prince

Augustus Frederick, his sixth son, with Lady Augusta Murray, daughter of the Earl of Dunmore. Both these marriages took place in Mayfair, though the ceremonies differed greatly.

George III never knew the exact details of the marriage of the Prince of Wales with Mrs Fitzherbert, as the secret was not fully revealed until 1905 when permission was granted to open a sealed packet deposited at Coutts Bank 72 years earlier. Inside was found the certificate of marriage between George Augustus, Prince of Wales, aged 23, and Mrs Mary Ann Fitzherbert aged 29, on December 15th, 1795, with two witnesses, though their signatures had been cut out. The protestant clergyman, the Rev. Robert Burt, who took the great risk of marrying them, was sworn to secrecy with a generous gift of money and the promise of preferment.

Mrs Fitzherbert's house where this most famous of all Mayfair's morganatic marriages took place – they knelt side by side in her drawing room behind locked doors – stood at the upper end of Park Street near Oxford Street. The house has been pulled down now, but one or two old houses still remain on the east side and Mrs Fitzherbert's was probably like one of these, small and unpretentious for those days; we can imagine the ardent Prince of Wales walking along the narrow cobbled street to his secret tryst on a cold December evening, as he came on foot all the way from Carlton House after nightfall to disarm suspicion, entering the back way through the stables and the garden.

There was to be no clandestine marriage in a locked drawing room in a back street at the Tyburn end of town for Prince Augustus Frederick, the Prince of Wales's younger brother. He brazenly chose St George's, Hanover Square, introducing himself to the Rector as 'Mr Augustus Frederick' explaining that he had married 'Miss Augusta Murray', when he was under age a few months before in Rome, and now they wanted to be married again for the sake of their child whose birth was imminent, as the clergyman himself could observe. For three Sundays in succession the banns were proclaimed between 'Mr Augustus Frederick and Miss Augusta Murray', and as no one saw 'any just cause or impediment' the two young people walked up the aisle of St George's on December 5th, 1793, like any other plain Mr and Miss, and were solemnly joined in holy matrimony, signing the register with the names they had given the parson, and without his having any idea that he was breaking the law. An attempt was made to prosecute the Rector and clergy of St George's when the secret of the unlawful marriage came out, but their innocence was obvious, and it only remained for the Court of Arches to annul the marriage by invoking the Royal Marriage Act – for the first time.

To return to the other erring couple, the Gloucesters; they did not remain in disgrace for long. After a spell of 'exile' in Italy where their second child, Prince William, was born in the Teodoli Palace in Rome in 1776, they returned home to Gloucester House, and were forgiven. This act of grace on the part of the King was due to the Duke's beautiful Duchess, Maria. By her tact, charm and impeccable behaviour as his brother's wife, the Duchess of Gloucester completely won over the King: the royal couple almost adopted their two young children, Princess Sophia and Prince William, and Queen Charlotte made a special pet of Prince William, nicknaming him Silly Billy.

Silly Billy spent most of his life in Mayfair: in his youth at Gloucester House, the home of his parents in Park Lane until his father's death when it was bought by Earl Grosvenor; then on his marriage with Princess Mary, King George III's daughter, in 1816, he bought Lord Elgin's house at the corner of Park Lane and Piccadilly which duly became known as Gloucester House, too, since he had succeeded to his father's title. But by then the old family house farther up Park Lane had changed its name from Gloucester House to Grosvenor House and was the home of the Grosvenor family.

At a period when the prestige of the Royal family had sunk to its lowest ebb, the Duke of Gloucester, Silly Billy, led a blameless life and always did his duty. As a young man he was sent on a goodwill mission to Scandinavia, Russia and Prussia, which he accomplished to the Government's satisfaction. He rose to be Field Marshal in the Army and was elected Chancellor of Cambridge University. At his installation as Chancellor he had the same form of remark for everyone he met: 'What college do you belong to?', 'How long have you been here?' and 'A very pretty breakfast'; with these safe questions he got through the ordeal. Thomas Raikes describes him as 'a quiet inoffensive character, rather tenacious of the respect due to his rank and strongly attached to the Tory party'. The priggish Stockmar considered his 'intellectual powers were not of a high order'. He wore a rather vacuous expression and was stout.

He was well aware of his nickname: when the Reform Bill was passed and knowing that King William had been in favour of it, he mischievously asked: 'Who's Silly Billy now?'

He was also known as Slice (of Gloucester Cheese).

He even did his duty by marrying, or rather not marrying. Satisfactory though his romance was with Princess Mary from the point of view of lineage – royalty marrying royalty – they had to wait many years for dynastic reasons. Silly Billy had to be kept in reserve for the Regent's daughter, and not until Prince Leopold had swept Princess Charlotte off were the two first cousins allowed to marry, by which time both were middle-aged – a poor reward for their virtue; and they had no children.

Their married home, Gloucester House at the corner of what is now Old Park Lane, faced Green Park with the garden of Buckingham Palace beyond. Built in the 1770s it was a modest-looking house with a charming green-roofed balcony on the first floor and, like nearly all houses lining Piccadilly, fronted by a long brick wall, with its entrance at the side in Park Lane.

A few years before the Duke bought his house from Lord Elgin, thousands of sightseers had flocked there to see the Elgin Marbles put on show in a Museum at the back: 'His Lordship's stoneshop', Byron jeered – 'where brawny brutes in stupid wonder stare . . .'

The Duke of Gloucester as an only son – his sister Princess Sophia died unmarried – inherited all the treasures from old Gloucester House: portraits of his beautiful mother, the Duchess of Gloucester, by Reynolds, Gainsborough and Francis Cotes: Benjamin West's picture of him and Princess Sophia hand in hand as children, painted at the request of the King, who suggested the addition of such incongruous details as the towers of Westminster Abbey and a lion's head in the background; together with an enormous quantity of furniture, silver and porcelain. The family of King George III and Queen Charlotte, originally fifteen, began to fail in the second generation and as the 'old' royal family died out, more royal possessions poured into Gloucester House, which became a storehouse of Hanoverian heirlooms.

Silly Billy – he kept his name until the end – died at Gloucester House in Piccadilly in 1834. After his death the house continued to be a royal residence as the home of his widow, the Duchess of Gloucester, a little old lady dressed in black taffeta and wearing a mob cap with streamers hanging down at the side who, as a little girl, had romped with her brothers and sisters and cousins on the lawns at Windsor. A great-great-granddaughter of King George I, she grew up in the 18th century, yet lived on into the second half of the nineteenth – into the reign of her niece, Queen Victoria. To enter her house in Piccadilly with its many pictures of the 'old' royal family was to step back over half a century to the days when her parents were on the throne. In the state drawing-room overlooking Piccadilly the Duchess kept one of her treasured possessions, a tall rosewood cabinet gleaming with geranium-coloured cups, saucers, plates, bulb baskets and an octagonal tea-pot; a hundred-piece tea set which the royal family presented to King George III on his Jubilee in 1809. The King and Queen and the royal family used this for breakfast on the morning of the Jubilee. Each piece was decorated with the eight-point star of the Order of the Garter and Garter plumes, the suggestion of the King's artistic daughter, Princess Elizabeth.

Four of the Duchess of Gloucester's brothers who had been present at that Royal Jubilee breakfast were still living in the eighteen-thirties: King William IV; Ernest Augustus, the King of Hanover; the Duke of Sussex, and the Duke of Cambridge. The 'good' Duke of Cambridge, as he was called (he was the only one of the royal dukes who led a blameless life), was her favourite and he lived only a little way up Piccadilly at Cambridge House[1] (now the Naval and Military Club), the elderly brother and sister giving a sunset glow of respectability to the dying Georgian age.

The scandals of the royal dukes were beginning to fade when past follies were unexpectedly called to mind by the news that the Duke of Sussex had married. The Duke was the same Prince Augustus Frederick, who as a youth had married Lady Augusta Murray at St George's. Now a 'widower', he chose St George's again and – history repeating itself thirty-seven years after his first marriage – he entered the church with a bride not of royal blood, who rejoiced in the names of Cecilia Letitia, the widow of Sir George Buggin of the City of London. Not being able to call herself Duchess of Sussex, she changed her name from Lady Cecilia Buggin to Lady Cecilia Underwood, which sounded more harmonious, assuming by sign manual her maternal surname, being the daughter of the 2nd Earl of Arran, who married a Miss Underwood.

His brother, King William IV, who as Duke of Clarence had lived for years with Mrs Jordan and had fathered a large family by her, was not one to invoke the Royal Marriage Act, and the morganatic marriage was allowed to run its course; and when Queen Victoria came to the throne she allowed her new aunt to style herself, not Her Royal Highness the Duchess of Sussex, but the Duchess of Inverness, after the Duke's second title, which immediately led to her being called 'Duchess Never-

[1] Built by Matthew Brettingham for Lord Egremont, 1756-60. Later home of Lord Palmerston.

theless'. The Duke was familiarly known as 'Uncle Buggin'. The difference in rank between them gave rise to embarrassing situations whenever the Queen was present, on which occasions the Duchess of Inverness, ex-Lady Buggin, had to be very careful where she stood and sat.

A portrait by T. Phillips of the unrepentant Duke of Sussex hangs in the Council Chamber of the Royal Society at Burlington House – he was elected its President in 1820 – and shows him with his favourite black silk skull cap on his head which he wore to keep his bald pate warm. He was the bane of all the tradesmen in the West End because of his habit of running up enormous bills, which, if the tradesmen were lucky, were settled every five years and only after repeated letters sent to his house-steward, Mr Stephenson at Kensington Palace, and many were not settled until after the Duke's death in 1843.

In the early years of her reign when Queen Victoria lived at Buckingham Palace she often visited her uncle and aunt in Piccadilly, and other friends in the West End. The greatest friend of her youth, Harriet, Duchess of Sutherland, her Mistress of the Robes for 24 years, lived very close at Stafford House in St James's. The house was the most magnificent in London and at a reception given by the Duchess, the young Queen paid her hostess a compliment worthy of Louis XIV: 'I have come from my house to your Palace'.

It was only after the Queen's widowhood and her retirement to Windsor that London saw so little of her; she seldom came to the West End except to drive through it in procession. She hardly knew Mayfair and once admitted to the Duke of Marlborough that she had never been in Curzon Street. Her visits were so rare that great excitement was caused one day towards the end of her reign when to the jingle of harness and clatter of hooves, and to everyone's surprise and delight, the Queen drove the length of Bond Street in an open landau preceded by equerries and outriders.

During the Queen's early married life, Buckingham Palace was included in St George's, and the Rector keeps in the vestry a small purple bound volume of baptisms performed in private houses within its boundaries – a list of very aristocratic infants – and among them are two of Queen Victoria's children, Princess Victoria and Princess Alice, both baptised in the private chapel of Buckingham Palace. The names of their parents and their place of residence are written in the book but the entry 'Quality of Parents' is left vacant. No more royal baptisms at Buckingham Palace are recorded as on the death of the Rector, Dr Hodgson, on October

9th, 1844, the parish of St George's was greatly reduced in size and the Palace no longer belonged to it.

As the Queen's family increased in numbers so assuring the succession, which at one time had seemed in danger, the links with the 'old' royal family became more and more tenuous, and every visit the Queen paid to her uncle and aunt in Piccadilly threatened to be the last. In 1850 the Duke of Cambridge died, leaving his sister, the Duchess of Gloucester, as the last survivor of all the brothers and sisters of the 'old' royal family – her 'Aunt Gloucester', as Queen Victoria called her in the quaint royal idiom. At last her time came to go and she died at Gloucester House on April 30th, 1857, aged 81, only a few days after the birth of Queen Victoria's last child, Princess Beatrice. Thus the two royal families, as it were, just touched.

The death of the Duchess of Gloucester still did not mean the end of the old house in Piccadilly and the dispersal of its treasures. It passed from one royal owner to another. The Duchess, having no children, chose as her heir Prince George, the son of her favourite brother, who had succeeded his father as Duke of Cambridge. To this young man who for two months before the birth of Queen Victoria was heir presumptive to the throne of Great Britain, hence his name George, she left Gloucester House in Piccadilly and all its contents – the pictures by Reynolds, Gainsborough and Cotes of the beautiful first Duchess of Gloucester, portraits of King George III and Queen Charlotte, and her brothers and sisters, Benjamin West's curious picture of Prince William and Princess Sophia of Gloucester, her furniture and knick-knacks, plate emblazoned with the royal arms, and the hundred-piece Jubilee Wedgwood service.

Few who passed the sleepy-looking old house with its green balcony and long brick wall shutting it off from Piccadilly knew of the romance in the life of its owner, the Duke of Cambridge, first cousin of the Queen, the dignified military figure who rose to be Commander-in-Chief of the British Army, his tunic glittering with medals and orders, and with the aura of Royal Highness about him.

All the Duke's uncles had been notorious for the scandals or irregularities of their private lives. No attempt had been made to hush them up – they had lived openly with their mistresses or unofficial 'wives'. But that was in the bad old days before the improving influence first of Queen Adelaide, and later of Queen Victoria and Prince Albert. When he was a boy, the Duke's name had been linked with Princess Victoria's, but neither party had shown much ardour. Instead Prince George, as he then was, fell in love with an actress at Drury Lane, Miss Louisa Fairbrother, and they married in 1847. He kept his marriage so secret that we know very little about it even now, for being 'a descendant of the body of His Majesty King George II', he had to ask permission of the sovereign to marry, and the royal assent had been neither sought nor granted.

Miss Fairbrother was not an actress in the tragic tradition of Mrs Siddons, or even like Mrs Jordan. She was more versatile, an *artiste* who excelled in pantomime, and one of her favourite parts was 'principal boy' in *Sinbad the Sailor*; a popular print of the eighteen-forties shows her arrayed in white diaphanous tights and a narrow striped jacket in the rôle of Sinbad with a jewelled scimitar in her belt and wearing a false black moustache and a tiny tuft of a beard in strange contrast with her long raven black hair tumbling down her swan-like neck. This curious picture hardly does credit to her great beauty; another portrait of her by Thomas Musgrove Joy shows her seated in a theatre box, probably Drury Lane – a delightful-looking woman with arched eyebrows and smiling mouth expressing her rare charm.

After her marriage she retired from the stage and settled down to domestic life. But she never lived at Gloucester House. When the secret at last came out, Queen Victoria strongly disapproved, but she did not try to annul the union by invoking the Royal Marriage Act, which would have been awkward as there were three sons. Instead, it was hushed up. The Duke never appeared with her on public occasions, and she was not entered in the reference books as his wife. She was given the name of Mrs FitzGeorge, and her three sons were also called FitzGeorge and debarred from succeeding to the Dukedom of Cambridge. This was Queen Victoria's ruling.

Unable to preside as Duchess of Cambridge at Gloucester House, Mrs FitzGeorge made a second home for herself and her husband not far away in Queen Street, in the heart of Mayfair, the short street leading off Curzon Street opposite Shepherd Market.

Mrs FitzGeorge's house, No. 6, Queen Street, still stands unaltered, and one can easily imagine the Duke of Cambridge alighting from his phaeton, which he drove himself, to seek relaxation there with his wife and children from the frozen grandeurs of Gloucester House. He always spent Sundays with his family, attending services at the Mayfair Chapel – one of the few occasions when they were ever seen in public together.

Fortunately Mrs FitzGeorge had no smouldering ambition to become a royal duchess, or even a non-royal duchess. She was quite content as the Duke's wife, living quietly in Queen Street, where she entertained her wide circle of friends including Mr Gladstone and Edward Lawson, the owner of the *Daily Telegraph*, later Lord Burnham, who wrote her obituary notice.

After nearly 50 years of married life Mrs FitzGeorge died in 1890, greatly mourned by her family and friends but hardly known to the world outside Queen Street. Queen Victoria, so far as is known, never met her, but she appears to have reconciled herself to her cousin's marriage to judge by the wistful entry the Duke of Cambridge made on the day his wife died: 'I received a most affectionate message from Her Majesty which I highly appreciate and which would have been such a joy to my beloved had she known the fact.'

The Duke of Cambridge survived his wife by many years and lived so long that the original lease bequeathed him by the Duchess of Gloucester ran out towards the end of his life. His son, Colonel Adolphus FitzGeorge, wrote to the ground landlord, the Ecclesiastical Commissioners, asking what terms they were asking for a new rent since his father, the Duke, did not want to move, having lived there such a long time and

> having followed the family of the Duke of Gloucester who owned the house for a considerable number of years previously. So that it has become a family house and he feels that as he is now getting old he would wish to finish his days in the house he knows so well and has lived in so long.

The Duke offered £59,700 for the reversion of the property. This was refused, and he then offered £2,000 a year rent. The Commissioners asked £2,700 and got it. The Duke was a rich man, owning property at Coombe Hill in Surrey besides his collection of valuable works of art. He died in 1904 aged 85, after living almost half a century at Gloucester House.

Soon after his death the old house which had stood at the corner of Piccadilly and Park Lane for nearly 150 years – during nearly half of which it had been in royal ownership – was demolished, and the present shiny white house with its green striped *Art Nouveau* gable was erected in its place, originally intended as a block of flats, the most luxurious and expensive in London. But later on it became an office block with motor showrooms on the street level. The new Gloucester House rose to the great height in those days of eight storeys and was considered a terrible eyesore. It was the first 'modern' building seen in Piccadilly.

King Edward VII objected to it strongly and summoned Lewis (Lulu) Harcourt, later Viscount Harcourt, who was First Commissioner of Works, to the Palace. He took him out into the garden and protested that the new block which bulked high over the trees ruined the outlook. He was unable to understand how his Commissioners of Works had allowed such a monstrosity to be erected. Harcourt replied that the new building had nothing whatever to do with His Majesty's Commissioners of Works, but that the responsibility lay with His Majesty's Ecclesiastical Commissioners, and that it was another very good reason for the dis-establishment of the Church.

The King, so Lord Harcourt related, was not overpleased with this reply.

King Edward VII, unlike Queen Victoria, was very fond of London and one cannot imagine the King saying he had never been in Curzon Street. He probably knew Mayfair a great deal better than many of its residents. In the eighteen-seventies he used to visit his boon companion, Christopher Sykes, at his handsome house at No. 11, Hill Street, until his generous host ruined himself in arranging sumptuous parties for his royal guest. His many millionaire friends invited him to their mansions in Park Lane . . . Sir Ernest Cassel at Brook House, Sir George Holford at Dorchester House, Lord Londonderry at Londonderry House. In Curzon Street itself he was often the guest of Lord and Lady Crewe at Crewe House and of the Marlboroughs at Sunderland House. Then there were his many lady friends: Mrs Arthur James who lived in Grafton Street, and Consuelo, Duchess of Manchester at 5, Grosvenor Square. And he often drove through Mayfair to visit Mrs George Keppel at 30, Portman Square on the other side of Oxford Street. He paid his visits discreetly, driving in the royal brougham through the quiet secluded streets which seemed a private part of London, still uncontaminated by the new century where old family state coaches, which had trundled out of Mayfair to the Abbey for his coronation, were stored away in dark stables.

After the Duke of Cambridge's death it was not until after the first World War that another member of the Royal Family settled in Mayfair. Great changes had come about and it was the period when many great houses were ending their long and illustrious history by being pulled down. It seemed, happily, as if this dismal process was being reversed when, in 1922, the Princess Royal and her husband, Lord Lascelles, took the most renowned of all the houses in Mayfair, if not in all of London: Chesterfield House, built by the great Earl of Chesterfield, the writer of the famous *Letters*. For a few years its many reception rooms blazed with lights, its grand staircase, up which Horace Walpole had often tripped, was thronged with guests, and the house fulfilled the function for which it had been built – that of a private town house. The Princess Royal's elder son, the Earl of Harewood, was born there. But its revival was short lived. It suffered the fate of most other great houses in Mayfair and when the Princess Royal and her family moved to 32, Green Street, off Park Lane, it was pulled down.

We have now arrived on the threshold of modern times – the inter-war period of King George V and Queen Mary. Queen Mary liked to shop in Bond Street and visit art exhibitions there, and her high maroon and gold royal Daimler was often seen in Mayfair, the Queen seated beside her lady-in-waiting bowing graciously to passers-by, carried along on a wave of emotion and loyalty that went rippling through the busy narrow streets.

Early in 1934 the royal Daimler was seen outside the house in Queen Street where Mrs FitzGeorge used to live. On her death the house had passed to her son, Sir Augustus FitzGeorge, and though the Old Masters had been sold (Gainsborough's portrait of Maria, Duchess of Gloucester fetched 12,705 guineas), many of the Duke of Cambridge's possessions from Gloucester House had found a second home in Queen Street. Sir Augustus lived there until his death in November, 1933, when the house stood empty. As *The Morning Post* of February 26th, 1934, wrote:

> . . . a treasure house of royal memories. . . . There are prints and portraits of every child of George III, each signed in the now faint signatures of those they depict – 'George', 'Will', 'Albert', can be deciphered. One print bears in clear decisive ink: 'Victoria'. And there is a portrait of the first [*sic*] Duchess of Cambridge with her children. In another room is the bed in which Mrs FitzGeorge died, once Miss Louisa Fairbrother, the morganatic wife of the Duke of Cambridge, who married her in defiance of Royal wishes. Upstairs a strange bed, adorned with rails and hangings to ward off mosquitos. It accompanied the soldier Duke on all his foreign campaigns. There are also the Duke's Garter and Orders, and gifts from ex-Kaiser William.

Queen Mary, the Duke of Cambridge's niece, visited the house in Queen Street to sort out the heirlooms and help decide their future.

Many are now in the Royal collections, and the others, including Benjamin West's double portrait of Prince William and Princess Sophia, and Francis Cotes' portrait of the first Duchess of Gloucester, and the Wedgwood Royal Jubilee set belong to the Duke of Cambridge's granddaughter, Princess Iris Galitzine *née* FitzGeorge.

Commercialisation was by now fast overtaking Mayfair as London moved westwards, and Bruton Street, so near to New Bond Street, lay in the direct line of advance. But before the avalanche broke over it, No. 17, the town house of the Earl and Countess of Strathmore, was the scene of a happy event when our present Queen was born there on April 21st, 1926. The birth of a child to the Duke and Duchess of York was a matter of great national concern, as even then it seemed likely that the baby, third in succession, would one day ascend the throne; and the Home Secretary, Sir William Joynson-Hicks, spent the night in Bruton Street, the last occasion of such a vigil at the birth of a royal child in the direct line of succession.

Later in the morning it was announced that 'Her Royal Highness the Duchess of York had given birth to a daughter', and amid great excitement the King and Queen drove up from Windsor to see their latest grandchild, their third. At one time the Duke and Duchess of York planned to take as their town house No. 40, Grosvenor Square, where Lady Oxford lived as a girl, but other counsels prevailed and 145, Piccadilly was chosen.

The Duke of Windsor as the young and charming Prince of Wales gave his royal patronage to Mayfair's night life, dancing into the small hours in the new night clubs which had sprung up there in the dance-crazy nineteen-twenties. It needed only for the Prince of Wales or his brother Prince George to visit a night club once or twice and it was made. The Embassy Club in Old Bond Street – it is still there – was the Prince of Wales' favourite, run by the incomparable Luigi Naintre, 'the friend of Kings', an Italian restaurateur who came from the East Room at the Criterion (followed by all the celebrities) and made the Embassy the most exclusive night club in London. The subscription was eight guineas a year with an entrance fee of twenty guineas.

But to call the Embassy a night club is misleading as it was very popular for luncheon or dinner, and much smarter than any hotel or restaurant. The Duke of Windsor in his memoirs *A King's Story* calls it 'The Buckingham Palace of night clubs'. Nevertheless, his staid father, King George V, thoroughly disapproved of his visits there, and nothing his eldest son said could make him alter his prejudice against night clubs which he imagined to be smoke-filled dens of iniquity.

Another of the Prince of Wales' haunts was 'Chez Victor' in Grafton Street next to the 'Grafton Galleries Club' where Paul Whiteman and his Band played. The Prince practically started 'Chez Victor' as he used to frequent the 'Grafton Galleries' (he was present with his three brothers on the evening when Paul Whiteman played there for the first time) and made a friend of Victor who ran it. One day the Prince said to him that if he wanted to open a place of his own he would patronise it. So Victor started up his own club 'Chez Victor' next door. It became the rage in 1927 with 'Hutch', then in his prime, singing *My Heart stood still* by Richard Rogers and Lorenz Hart at the same time as he was performing as a 'speciality pianist' in *One Damned Thing after Another* at the London Pavilion.

'Uncle's' at 13, Albemarle Street, was another favourite with the Prince of Wales. Like 'Chez Victor' it stayed open much longer than the Embassy and the Prince would dance there after attending a formal party and not return to York House, St James's, until dawn was breaking over London.

A house in Mayfair demolished in 1933 must be mentioned as it belongs to history: 21, Grosvenor Square, where the Prince of Wales met his future wife. There are many stories about the Duke of Windsor's first meeting with Mrs Simpson, but Thelma, Lady Furness, who introduced them, should know. In her twin autobiography, *Double Exposure*, which she wrote with her sister, Consuelo Vanderbilt, she relates that an impromptu party was in progress at her house in Grosvenor Square with Mrs Simpson as one of the guests when the Prince of Wales paid an unexpected call, and she introduced him to 'Wallis' in her drawing room upstairs. She gives the date as 'the latter part of 1930 or early 1931'.

No. 21, which belonged to her husband's family, stood at the corner of Grosvenor Square next to the old Italian Embassy before it moved across the square. Both houses were pulled down to make way for the large corner block of flats where General Eisenhower had his Army Headquarters in the early part of the last war as a plaque on the front informs us, almost on the spot where the introduction took place, which a few years later was to lead to the Abdication.

King George VI would have returned to Mayfair if Buckingham Palace had been destroyed by bombing, as an emergency bomb-proof flat was kept for him on the fourth floor of the Ministry of Education building clamped on to the back of old Lansdowne House. It was never needed. Instead, when the war was over, it became the home of Princess Marie Louise, who moved there from Schomberg House in Pall Mall where she lived with her sister, Princess Helena. Here the Princess, who was a granddaughter of Queen Victoria, kept her collection of Napoleon relics – now on loan to the Hove Museum of Art – and entertained her many friends. She spent the last years of her long life writing her memoirs which she completed shortly before she died in 1957, the last member of the royal family to live in Mayfair. With her death ended a historic connection which had begun when Princess Anne moved into Berkeley House before ascending the throne – a span of over 250 years.

28. Mrs FitzGeorge. Mrs FitzGeorge at the time of her marriage, by Thomas Musgrave Joy. (Collection of Princess Iris Galitzine)

29. Miss Louisa Fairbrother. Miss Louisa Fairbrother, later Mrs FitzGeorge, was an actress at Drury Lane before she married George, Duke of Cambridge. She took the part of Sinbad in *Sinbad the Sailor*. (Collection of Mrs David Porter)

30. MAYFAIR SKYLINE. King Edward VII called Gloucester House at the corner of Piccadilly and Old Park Lane a monstrosity because it ruined the view from Buckingham Palace. Today the 25-storey Hilton Hotel soars up behind it.

31. CHESTERFIELD HOUSE. The 4th Earl of Chesterfield was the first to build a large house overlooking Hyde Park. His magnificent palace built in 1750 was later the home of Princess Mary and the Earl of Harewood. (National Monuments Record)

CHAPTER SIX

Park Lane

PARK LANE, Mayfair's western frontier, presents a line of tall massive buildings to the Park, huge blocks of flats alternating with hotels now dwarfed by the London Hilton, which shoots up its slender tower like a rocket near Hyde Park Corner.

Contrast this battlemented front with the same view in mid-18th century when the east-west streets of Mayfair had just reached the edge of Hyde Park ending rather lamely where Tyburn Lane, no more than a narrow track, meandered down to Hyde Park Corner, hugging the Park wall.

The only impressive house in sight was Lord Chesterfield's new mansion – *London in Miniature* of 1755 calls it 'a most superb and magnificent edifice' – built on open land near Shepherd Market where the fair was still held every first of May, with the squat bell tower of the Mayfair Chapel seen over the roofs. Curzon Street was already laid out and creeping towards the Park, but it was unpaved and with houses only along the southern side, as the garden of Chesterfield House stretched down the northern side as far as Mr Shepherd's long 'white garden house', now Crewe House.

Lord Chesterfield was a pioneer in two respects. He left his house in Grosvenor Square to come to this wild west part of London, jokingly telling his friends, who were surprised at his having chosen so desolate a place, that he would have to keep a house dog; and what was still more enterprising, he commissioned his architect, Isaac Ware, to site his new house facing the Park, which was not then the tidy, cultivated and policed open space it is today, but an extension of the country infested by vagabonds. He began to build about 1747, and two years later, in one of his celebrated letters to his friend Dayrolles, he writes:

I have yet finished nothing but my Boudoir and my Library; the former is the gayest and most cheerful room in England; the latter the best. My garden is now turfed, planted and sown, and will in two months more make a scene of verdure and flowers not common in London.

Chesterfield House with its spacious forecourt and its side pavilions linked to the central block by segmental colonnades corresponded to the continental idea of a nobleman's house, and the French traveller Pierre Jean Grosley,[1] who visited England in 1765, named it one of the few London houses he saw which could be compared to an '*hôtel*' in Paris. It had six reception rooms on the ground floor, and its grand staircase, brought from Canons, was of palatial dimensions, the entwined 'C's of the ironwork balustrade, originally the initial of the Duke of Chandos, conveniently suiting the name of its new owner.

The 6th Lord Chesterfield, a famous sportsman, let the house in 1850, and it was sold in 1869 when its decline started. Its new owner Mr Charles Magniac M.P., who paid £150,000 for the house, recouped himself by selling off the garden at the back and pulling down the side pavilions. Though surrounded by new houses, it still looked a stately mansion seen from Stanhope Gate, and Lord Burton, the brewer, who bought it after Magniac went bankrupt, spent a fortune on restoring it to its former glories, until it finally fell a victim to development after the Princess Royal and Lord Harewood moved out in 1932.

Crewe House, originally Edward Shepherd's 'white garden house', still has a rural air about it, standing a little back from Curzon Street behind its well-tended lawn and tall plane trees. Shepherd, having made his fortune developing this part of Mayfair, died here in 1747. Rebuilt in late Georgian times, the house passed into the hand of James Archibald, first Baron Wharncliffe, the great-grandson of Lady Mary Wortley Montagu and editor of her letters, who bought the 999 year lease in 1818 for £12,000 when it became known as Wharncliffe House. By the end of the century, as Curzon Street became more fashionable, its value had increased considerably and it was sold to the Marquess of Crewe, statesman and diplomat, for £90,000, when it changed its name again, to Crewe House. Its entrance used to be through the garden at the back, now built over, but this was changed by Lord Crewe who removed a conservatory and built the present front entrance from Curzon Street.

[1] Austin Dobson in *Eighteenth-Century Vignettes*, Third Series, devotes an informative essay to Grosley's *Londres*, published in Lausanne in 1770.

It served many purposes during his ownership of nearly fifty years. In the first World War he offered it to the government and it was taken over as the headquarters for propaganda to enemy countries under the direction of Lord Northcliffe who was dubbed by the Germans 'The Minister for the Destruction of German Confidence'. After the war when Lord Crewe was British Ambassador in Paris it was let to two successive American ambassadors, Frank B. Kellogg and Alanson B. Houghton, because there was no official residence attached to the United States Embassy in London at this time, and ambassadors had to make their own arrangements.

Now Crewe House belongs to Thomas Tilling Ltd., to whom we owe thanks for keeping the long low house so white and the lawns so smooth and for floodlighting it at night winter and summer. Seen through the trees from Curzon Street, Crewe House has a dreamy romantic look about it, taking us back to the days of Thackeray's May Fair when it stood 'over against the Chapel'.

Mr Beresford Chancellor in his book *The Private Palaces of London* published in 1908 included Crewe House as the smallest of the eight mansions in Mayfair although it had eighteen bedrooms and numerous reception rooms. Now it is one of the last three survivors with Apsley House and the much mutilated Lansdowne House: the other five, Devonshire House, Chesterfield House, Londonderry House, Dorchester House and Grosvenor House have been demolished over the years.

Apsley House takes its name from Lord Apsley who, twenty years after Lord Chesterfield had settled on the west side of Mayfair, built himself a fine house at Hyde Park Corner, then an outpost of London where a cluster of inns served the needs of the cattle drovers who attended the various London markets. Wearing its jacket of red brick, Apsley House, later to be known as 'No. 1, London' when the great Duke of Wellington lived there, stood near the turnpike. It was the most westerly of a long line of houses stretching in a graceful curve along the southern frontier of Mayfair as far as Devonshire House, with the twin towers of Westminster Abbey seen in the distance over the trees of Green Park.

Park Lane, as Tyburn Lane was called after the gallows were removed to Newgate, could offer no such fair sweep. Except where Chesterfield House faced the Park, Mayfair only turned the jagged ends of its streets towards the west. But gradually the elegant world, following Lord Chesterfield's example, started to build houses facing the Park, and in the early years of the 19th century we can watch the list of Park Lane residents in Boyle's Court Guide grow longer and longer as this side of Mayfair was chosen by the *bon ton*.

As London expanded westwards in early Victorian days, the two new residential districts of Tyburnia and Belgravia grew up to the north-west and south-west of Mayfair. Divided by Hyde Park, their only connecting link was Park Lane, which was quite unfitted to carry the heavy north-south traffic. The congestion of vehicles passing up and down its narrow length became chaotic after Victoria Station was opened in the year 1860, as Park Lane was the only direct route between the new station and Paddington, public vehicles being prohibited from entering Hyde Park. The conditions were worst at the Piccadilly end where it tapered down to a narrow gulley by Gloucester House, where the Duke of Cambridge lived. Here heavy growlers, nimble hansoms, the huge red Paddington-Victoria bus, costermongers' donkey-carts, lumbering coal carts, and sumptuous private carriages with coachmen and 'Tiger' on the box, became wedged in an inextricable mass of traffic. There was no rule of the road, and no traffic policemen as we understand them. To make the congestion and confusion worse, it was quite common for a herd of cattle to be driven along Park Lane on the way to one of London's markets, and the cows and sheep, maddened by the shouts and the crack-ing of whips, charged into the *mêlée*, overturning lighter vehicles and scattering any pedestrians foolhardy enough to try to cross the road. The Piccadilly bottle-neck was one of the sights of London to be shown to country visitors, especially at peak times of the year during the season and at Christmas.

As the chaos in Park Lane grew worse, public indignation mounted, and angry people who had lost their trains or missed their dinners, wrote to the papers. To many the obvious solution was to pull down Gloucester House. It was one thing to make the suggestion, another to carry it out. The Duke of Cambridge, a cousin of the Queen, was a formidable person to evict from his house for the sake of eliminating a bottle-neck.

An alternative was put forward by 'A Sufferer' in a letter to *The Times* on July 14th, 1864. After enumerating the four accidents which had occurred the previous day he suggested the opening-up of Hamilton Place, then closed at its northern end, and introducing one-way traffic (though he did not use the term) – the upward flow to use Hamilton Place and the down traffic to use the lower end of Park Lane.

Immediately the residents of the few large houses in Hamilton Place, built by Robert Adam in 1805, were up in arms. They objected violently to the idea of having the peace of their cul-de-sac disturbed, and put up a stout fight, backed by some high-sounding names. For years the battle raged between the two parties: one for pulling down Gloucester House, the other for piercing Hamilton Place.

The Duke of Cambridge rallied powerful allies, among them Delane, Editor of *The Times*, and the affair was debated in Parliament, the result being that Gloucester House was saved, and Hamilton Place was pierced – and widened – by Act of Parliament, and the new street opened to one-way traffic in 1871. A cartoon in *Vanity Fair* of 1870, showing the Duke of Cambridge driving his phaeton and entitled 'A Military Difficulty', refers to this battle royal.

A familiar Park Lane landmark used to stand at the northern end of Hamilton Place: the Poets' Fountain by Thornycroft, erected in 1875, which has a curious story. It was the gift of a certain Mrs Marian Browne, who died intestate and without heirs, and so all her considerable fortune went to the state. It was known, however, that she wished a fountain to be erected at this spot and £5,000 of her estate was set aside by the Government to be spent on it. The fountain was shaped like a three tiered Victorian wedding cake, with the figures of tragedy, comedy and poetry on the lower tier; the statues of Chaucer, Milton and Shakespeare on the upper; and aloft, the sprightly figure of Fame blowing a trumpet.

The fountain recalled the time when the two streams of stately horse-drawn traffic divided at this point, but in the motor age it became an obstruction and was removed in the nineteen-thirties. So far as can be ascertained, it was not set up elsewhere – one more Mayfair monument which has disappeared without trace.

The two streets about which there was such a fuss a hundred years ago are now deserted since the building of the new Park Lane, and the gulley known as Old Park Lane, the scene of the notorious bottle-neck, is so quiet that without any risk to life or limb one can pace out its width – 30 feet from pavement edge to pavement edge. Through this narrow gap in Piccadilly all the north-south traffic had to pass a hundred years ago – one can understand why there was such chaos.

Park Lane has been replanned since those days, and it has carved out for itself a new channel which comes sweeping through 'Piccadilly Terrace', the line of Victorian mansions which used to stretch from the corner of Hamilton Place to Apsley House. It was known as Rothschild Row because so many members of the Rothschild family lived there: Miss Alice de Rothschild at 142, Baron Ferdinand at 143, Baron Albert at 145 and Baron Lionel de Rothschild at 147 and 148, whose double house was actually joined to Apsley House at 149, Piccadilly.

The bombed remains of 145, Piccadilly – George VI's house before he became King – and its neighbours to the west, 146–148, Piccadilly, have been swept away leaving Apsley House isolated. The old house, faced with honey-coloured Bath stone, looks perhaps more imposing on its island site, but being sliced off from its neighbours it cannot live up to its historic name of 'No. 1 London' any more, and Hyde Park Corner is a corner no longer; it is a whirligig of traffic honeycombed with tunnels called Duke of Wellington Place.

Londonderry House, the famous Park Lane mansion which stood at the corner of Hertford Street, was demolished in 1965. Though modest in appearance (by Park Lane standards) it nevertheless contained rooms of the utmost magnificence. The 3rd Marquess of Londonderry, half-brother of the celebrated politician, Lord Castlereagh, married one of the greatest heiresses of the day, Lady Frances Anne Vane-Tempest and with her money he bought old Holdernesse House and rebuilt it regardless of expense in 1824. In the four decades that followed Holdernesse House, as it continued to be known until 1872, was the scene of splendid entertainments given by Frances Anne, one of the great Tory hostesses, and again in Edwardian days when the 6th Marquess entertained here on a grand scale.

After the first World War Londonderry House succeeded Lansdowne House as the official meeting place for the Conservative party, and became famous for the receptions held on the eve of the opening of Parliament by Lord and Lady Londonderry, who, with the Party leader standing at their side, received the hundreds of prominent guests who crowded up the gilded staircase.

This historic London house managed to survive during the decade after the last war, but no longer as a private residence. Even before the war it had cost £3,000 a year to run, and the only possible way to maintain it was to let it out for wedding receptions, dress shows and various publicity ventures. These 'open days' gave many people the opportunity of seeing the sumptuous interior and the magnificent collection of heroic-sized pictures lining the ballroom formed by the 3rd Marquess to which portraits by Sargent, de Laszlo and Lavery had been added.

The house was finally sold in 1963, and the new Londonderry House Hotel has arisen on the site, cheek by jowl with the Hilton Hotel.

Nowadays it is more interesting to explore the narrow streets leading off Park Lane into the interior of Mayfair and Shepherd Market than to keep to Park Lane itself, which has become one long wall of red brick stretching in an almost unbroken line from Hyde Park Corner to Marble Arch.

The first street on the right, Hertford Street leading to Shepherd Market, used to be a cart track winding down to Brookfield and the fair-ground from Hyde Park Corner. It became one of the most fashionable streets in London, so near the Park, in the early eighteen-thirties. Bulwer-Lytton lived there then, though he has no plaque; but there are two other plaques, both on the same house, No. 11, which was the home of General John Burgoyne, the unsuccessful hero of the War of American Independence, and of Richard Brinsley Sheridan, the playwright. Lord Sandwich, famous for his musical parties, and Charles Hawtrey, the actor, also lived at No. 11, Hertford Street.

Still keeping to the back streets we can take a short cut into Curzon Street either through the hole in the wall in Pitts Head Mews or by following along narrow Derby Street, which takes us out opposite Chesterfield House, alas new Chesterfield House, a block of flats with the same name on the site of the old mansion.

Curzon Street used to stop short at the corner of South Audley Street and, being so wide and shut off at the other end, became a fashionable place in which to live. A few of the remaining smaller Park Lane houses stand at the corner where Curzon Street now joins Park Lane, with their entrances in Curzon Place, formerly Seamore Place. Their curving fronts or, to be exact, their backs overlooking the Park are spoilt by the row of unsightly one-storey shops built out on the pavement which should be scraped off, being unworthy of the new Park Lane. There are better examples farther up, their bow windows and barrel-shaped balconies gleaming in the sun like the Regency houses on the front at Brighton, the sequence Nos. 94–99 being particularly fine with trees and well-kept flower beds at the edge of the pavement.

Grosvenor House, the home of the Duke of Westminster, the landlord of nearly half of Mayfair, stood at the corner of Upper Grosvenor Street and Park Lane, occupying two-and-three-quarter acres, its garden running down to Mount Street. It was the first Duke of Gloucester's house enlarged and embellished, and it was entered from Upper Grosvenor Street through a magnificent colonnaded screen 110 feet long, built by Thomas Cundy, with tall ornamental gates at either end for carriages.

The Duke of Westminster possessed one of the finest collections of Old Masters in England, begun by Richard the 1st Earl Grosvenor and augmented by his son and grandson. The collection included masterpieces by Titian, Van Dyck, Rubens, Rembrandt, Hogarth, Gainsborough's *Blue Boy* and Sir Joshua Reynolds' *Sarah Siddons*. They were hung in a large picture gallery built in 1827 – also by Cundy – as the western wing of Grosvenor House next to Park Lane.

Lord Duveen used to tell the story of how he bought the *Blue Boy* from the Duke. He was crossing the Atlantic in 1921, and on board the *Aquitania* with him were Mr H. E. Huntington, the American millionaire, and his wife, who were occupying the Gainsborough suite hung with copies of his masterpieces. 'Who's the boy in the blue suit?' Huntington asked Duveen, and hearing it was Gainsborough's finest and most famous painting he asked where the original was. Duveen told him. 'How much is it?' Huntington asked. Duveen told him he did not think it could be had for any price, as it was the greatest of English masterpieces. 'What would be the price if it ever *were* sold?' Huntington asked. Duveen hesitated and quoted the figure of 600,000 dollars (about £120,000). Huntington was tempted. After a call to see the Duke of Westminster Duveen did not find it difficult to persuade him to part not only with the *Blue Boy*, but with *Sarah Siddons* and *The Cottage Door* by Gainsborough at a price only slightly more than the one he quoted to Huntington. He delivered the *Blue Boy* personally to Huntington in Paris for 620,000 dollars, and eventually sold him the other two masterpieces as well, making a very nice profit.

Now all the magnificent collection of pictures has been dispersed, and the site of Grosvenor House, which was demolished in 1926, is occupied by the hotel of the same name.

The only rival to Grosvenor House in Park Lane was Dorchester House, built with walls three-and-a-half-feet thick in imitation of an Italian Renaissance *palazzo*, for Mr R. S. Holford by Vulliamy in 1852 on land bought from the Dean and Chapter of Westminster for £45,000. It occupied the island site on which the Dorchester Hotel now stands, and took its name from the Earls of Dorchester, who lived in an earlier house there. This retention of the old name by a town house seems to be a London tradition.

Dorchester House had the finest staircase of any private palace in

London after Stafford House, and in Victorian days great London houses were known by their staircases. Mounting a crowded staircase could take as long as half an hour while the resplendent major-domo with powdered hair bawled out the names of the hundreds of guests to the host and hostess standing at the head. Sydney Smith has described in ecstatic language the sensation of mounting a great staircase at a grand reception, and there were few staircases of London mansions he did not know:

> An immense square with trees flowering with flambeaux, with gas for grass and every window illuminated with countless chandeliers, and voices reiterating for ever and ever: Sydney Smith is coming upstairs.

Dorchester House was built a little after his time, but he would have appreciated its marble staircase, which took up the centre of the house and cost £30,000, leading up by easy flights to the arcaded gallery which in turn opened into one room grander than the last – the Saloon, the Green Drawing Room, the Red Drawing Room and the State Drawing Room, all elaborately decorated by Italian artists and with magnificent marble chimney-pieces designed by Alfred Stevens, the 'English Michelangelo'.

Dorchester House was often let by its last owner Sir George Holford who was equerry to King Edward VII. The Shah of Persia took the enormous house in 1895 and London was flooded with stories about the eastern potentate's original views on politics. According to one report the Shah had been much perturbed by the downfall of the Government and had at once offered his Afghan escort for the protection of the Royal family, and expressed his intention of being present at the execution of Lord Rosebery.

Another notable tenant of Dorchester House was the United States Ambassador, Mr Whitelaw Reid, who had a liking for grand London houses. As the special representative of his country at Queen Victoria's Diamond Jubilee he took Lord Lonsdale's house in Carlton House Terrace, and for King Edward's coronation he rented Brook House in Park Lane, reputedly at £100 a day, from Lord Tweedmouth – for a coronation which had to be postponed owing to King Edward's last-minute operation for appendicitis.

The housing of America's representatives abroad can give rise to bitter controversy and Mr Whitelaw Reid's choice of Dorchester House – though he paid the rent of 4,500 guineas a year out of his own pocket – caused a furore in America, but he found a loyal supporter in both

President 'Teddy' Roosevelt and Secretary of State John Hay. 'As for those criticisms of your method of life – all I hope is that they bother you as little as they bother me,' wrote the President.

Mr Whitelaw Reid, who carried on his official business at the drab U.S. Embassy in Victoria Street, gave magnificent receptions in the sumptuous surroundings of Dorchester House, which he described in letters home to Mrs Theodore Roosevelt, notably the account of a dinner he gave for King Edward VII, when about fifty people came in afterwards for some music provided by 'Caruso and others'. Reading this we are transported back to the opulent days before 1914 when the greatest artists like Caruso or Melba would be brought to London by steamer and train to sing a few songs for a princely fee before a room full of guests who might not be particularly musical.

The famous eagle which spreads its wings over Grosvenor Square from the roof of the United States Embassy had a predecessor in London. Mr Whitelaw Reid on a journey to Rome happened to see a fine spread eagle carved in marble which took his fancy. He bought it thinking it would look well in the grounds of his country house, but after getting it to London he had the idea of mounting it over the main entrance of Dorchester House where the noble bird seemed to be poising its wings for a flight down Park Lane. Its wings were six feet from tip to tip.

This well known and popular American ambassador in London died in office at Dorchester House in 1912.

At the corner of Upper Grosvenor Street we can see Disraeli's house, or rather the house which belonged to his rich wife, the widow of Wyndham Lewis, who kept the careful accounts. Mary Anne made him very comfortable here, waiting up for him always, with lights gleaming from the windows, when he returned from the House.

We can explore another side street farther up, Culross Street, which has graduated from a mews. Now the stables have been converted into charming little houses, their doors and windows painted yellow or blue, their fronts gay with window boxes and tubs of flowers, and letting at enormous prices. The compact four-storey red brick house on the left, No. 4, almost touching the back of the American Embassy, might be a Georgian house in a country town, its sash windows still complete with their original glazing bars, and its elegant white-framed front door approached by a few steps. It probably started life as a coachman's house. No. 1, on the opposite side, was the home of the Duke of Westminster's butler. After the first World War the bell rang one day and the caller asked if there were lodgings to be had, as the Duke's butler always used to oblige in this way, but the new tenant, an American woman, could not help.

Walking back to Park Lane we pass on the right a high iron arch supporting a lantern: the entrance to the stables of Dudley House, the last survivor of the Park Lane mansions. The house, No. 100, Park Lane with its glass-fronted loggia surmounted by the Dudley arms, directly faces the Park, and was built by the eccentric Earl of Dudley, about whom so many anecdotes are told. In its heyday Dudley House had six kitchens in the basement and needed a staff of 100 servants. The panelled rooms, now converted to offices, bear witness to its opulent past, among them the cream and gold picture gallery where the famous Dudley art collection (sold at Christie's in 1892) could be seen, as old Baedekers quaintly worded it, 'by applying in writing to the Earl's secretary'. The ballroom was upstairs, but it was bombed during the last war and only the parquet floor remains. Dudley House once belonged to Sir Joseph Robinson, a multi-millionaire who arrived in Park Lane via the Kimberley diamond fields, and Mrs James Corrigan took it in 1939 at a rent of £5,000 for two months.

At the corner of Upper Brook Street there is a unique view of Mayfair. We can see right across the famous parallelogram at almost its widest point, and with field glasses we could read the words 'Dickins and Jones' on the large shop at the far end of the vista which stretches as far as Regent Street.

Woods Mews, the next side street, used to be lined with stables as this was the centre of 'Livery Mayfair', being on the edge of the Park, and the large red brick building on the left with the wide gate is a well-preserved example of a Victorian stable yard. The date 1887 is carved above the imposing entrance which leads into the yard where stable boys used to groom their horses and wash down the gleaming barouches. It is now a garage, but the old stable clock still tells the time.

A century ago Mayfair abounded in stables, and the livery population of coachmen, stable boys, yard helpers, harness cleaners and grooms was estimated at more than two thousand. There were also establishments known as 'Job Masters' which stabled horses for riding in the Row and had enough mounts for a regiment. The smell of horse dung on a hot day in mid-summer must have been appalling. (In 1851 according to Murray's *Modern London*, London counted 40,000 horses.)

This north-west corner of Mayfair had its quota of saddlers, the most famous being Whippy's at 35, North Audley Street where the Duke of Wellington bought his saddles and riding equipment from Salamanca to Waterloo. When Haydon was painting his picture of the Duke on Copenhagen he was unable to obtain the original Waterloo saddle, which had been eaten by mice many years before, but Whippy's obliged by supplying him with a replica and other accoutrements. Their fine Regency shop-front was demolished in 1908.

On the other side of the street the Regency stucco front next to St Mark's Rectory, numbered 11 and 12, North Audley Street, conceals a charming early Georgian house which goes back to 1730 and even earlier if we accept the story that the Countess of Suffolk, the intelligent mistress of King George II, lived here. But neither this nor the tradition that the house was designed by the Earl of Burlington at the King's expense are proved by facts.

We do know, however, that Colonel Ligonier owned the house from 1730 until his death in 1771. He was of Huguenot extraction and rose to be Commander-in-Chief of the British Army and was made an Earl. The *London Chronicle* of December 15th–17th, 1757, reported that the Colonel who commanded the First Regiment of Foot Guards 'gave a grand entertainment at his house in North Awdley Street to all the officers of the Regiment'.

It is a pity that the Colonel's party did not take place in the summer as at the back of the house there is a beautifully proportioned room, the Long Gallery, with a coffered dome picked out in Wedgwood blue which opens out on a delightful courtyard garden. Hemmed in by tall buildings and invisible from outside, the garden is laid out in formal style with lead statues, shaded by planes, poplars and an old fig tree which droops its branches over an ornamental pond. Two sphinxes keep watch under the windows.

The house has been in private hands since Colonel Ligonier's day, and it is thanks to two of its owners, both women, that it has not been demolished. In 1890 Lady Louisa Wells, whose lease was about to end, fell dangerously ill, and her doctor held out no hope of recovery. She was 60. As the house was due for demolition the Duke of Westminster, her landlord, wrote to her that she need not worry about her lease coming to an end as she could stay there for the rest of her life. She miraculously recovered, and lived to be a nonagenarian, by which time the proper artistic value of the house was beginning to be appreciated. At tea time Lady Louisa always sat by the richly carved marbled chimney-piece in the Long Gallery, surrounded by her silver knick-knacks arranged on little tables. She used an ear-trumpet and it was the delight of one of her great-grandnephews to stuff it with a selection of her minute silver treasures. On Lady Louisa's death in the 1920s Lord Ivor Churchill took the house and restored it to its former splendour. Nevertheless, after the last war the threat of demolition returned, and, but for the action of the present owner, Christabel Lady Aberconway, it might well have been demolished by now. Her lease was coming to an end and she offered a capital sum to the Grosvenor Estate in return for a further 99 years. This was refused. The second Duke of Westminster was a friend of hers and she appealed to him. He accepted her offer and now it looks as if this Georgian house with its charming garden will be reasonably safe for several more generations.

Lady Aberconway's predecessor was Mr Samuel Courtauld, the patron of the arts, and she actually found the house for him which partly explains why he bequeathed the remainder of its lease to her in 1947. He also left her the two urns which decorate the niches at either end of the Long Gallery which were designed for him by Rex Whistler in 1934. One urn is carved with the nine muses, and the other with eight famous Samuels chosen by Lady Aberconway. The swarm of Sams are the Prophet Samuel, Samuel Johnson, Samuel Butler, Samuel Richardson, Samuel Pepys, Samuel Scott, Samuel Rogers and Samuel Coleridge, all grouped round the entwined initials of the ninth Sam – Samuel Courtauld.

Several French impressionist paintings collected by Samuel Courtauld still hang in the house, giving the exquisitely furnished interior a special distinction. This house in North Audley Street and Lady Illingworth's in nearby Grosvenor Square, built within a few years of each other, recall the time when all the large houses in Mayfair were private residences before the wave of commercialisation turned them into offices, clubs, shops, beauty salons, banks and casinos.

Now to return to Park Lane along that avenue of red-brick Mayfair, Green Street, where the small side turnings lead to former mews and coach houses. The large stable population of Mayfair recalls a story told of Mr Alfred Beit, the South African millionaire, who came to live in Park Lane in 1896. He built his house almost next door (if one can use such an expression in Park Lane) to Grosvenor House, leasing the site from the Duke of Westminster. The Duke, worried about the type of house that Mr Beit intended to build, had a note sent round to him on the eve of signing the lease, urgently insisting that he should spend at least £10,000 on it. Mr. Beit, who liked riding in the Row and always drove to the City in his brougham and pair, replied that he was intending to spend £10,000 on the stables alone. His house, now vanished, was a long low building on an island site, described as a cross between a glorified bungalow and a dwarf Tudor grange. Born in Hamburg, he was much addicted to the idea of a winter garden, and he added a single storey extension in which there was a large rockery, tropical plants and a pond. This exotic London house was occupied after his death in 1906 by the Hon. Frederick Guest, and renamed Aldford House, and was sold for £80,000 for redevelopment in 1931, when the present block of flats, Aldford House, was built on the site betweeen South Street and Aldford Street.

Of all the multi-millionaires who lived in Park Lane the best known was Sir Ernest Cassel, the friend of King Edward VII, who moved here from 48, Grosvenor Square when he bought Brook House from Lord Tweedmouth. Built by T. H. Wyatt, the architect of Knightsbridge Barracks, in 1867, Brook House dominated the corner of Brook Street and Park Lane, and was considered to violate every tradition of this decorous neighbourhood. Not only was it immensely tall (for those days) but it was built in the now familiar red brick with stone dressings in a street lined with stucco fronted houses.

Sir Ernest Cassel spent a fortune on it, importing 800 tons of marble from Italy for the grand staircase, hall and galleries. On his death it passed to his granddaughter, Lady Mountbatten, and was demolished in 1931 to make way for the present block of flats which has a two-storey penthouse six floors up where Lord and Lady Mountbatten used to live.

The Park Lane millionaires did not like houses of the conventional type and indulged their fancy in styles of the past, like Mr R. W. Hudson, the soap king, who built himself a mediaeval folly, Stanhope House, decorated with heraldic shields and gargoyles, his cult of the past even making him prefer narrow gothic windows which restrict the glorious view of the Park. This quaint house – the work of W. H. Romaine Walker – by some miracle still stands at the corner of Stanhope Street opposite the Dorchester Hotel. The ground floor is occupied by the Park Lane branch of Barclays Bank, which has entered into the gothic spirit by inscribing its name in 'Olde Worlde' gold lettering on the front. The mediaeval house seems almost incomplete without a moat.

Across the road stood – until a few years ago – another architectural vagary, the house which Mr Barney Barnato, the South African millionaire, built in imitation of a French château, its roof lined with statues. He died before it was completed and it was bought by Sir Edward Sassoon, who banished the statues (to Preston Park in Brighton) and made it a treasure house of 18th-century furniture and pictures, installing exquisite rococo panelling from the Palffy Palace in Vienna.

The presence of all these multi-millionaires living in their sumptuous houses cheek by jowl in Park Lane provided sitting targets for the tub-thumpers of Speaker's Corner at Marble Arch, and in the years of depression after the first World War they needed only to point through the trees at the mansions of the 'bloated plutocrats', making them responsible for all the evils of the times.

The post war slump was the death blow to the big houses in Park Lane whether home of peer or merchant prince. Notices, 'For Sale' and 'To Let', went up everywhere, and dust settled on marble staircases and deserted ballrooms. When no buyer seemed interested the demolition men moved in, and one great house after another came crashing down – after Grosvenor House came Dorchester House, which, like Clarendon House, was built and swept away in one lifetime. Flames leapt high from the vacant sites as floorboards and, alas, precious panelling fed the bonfires, which gave out their pungent resinous smell like funeral pyres.

Within ten years Park Lane was transformed from a road lined with private houses, each one different from the other – some very grand, others modest – to a thoroughfare of American-style blocks of flats and huge hotels, soaring above the trees of Hyde Park.

Was all this destruction necessary? The answer must be 'yes', if London were to enter the mid-twentieth century as a modern city. Park Lane enjoys the finest position in London, overlooking Hyde Park, and the alternative for it was to become a museum street, and the standard of architecture did not warrant that. But the cost of new Park Lane has nevertheless been high, and the destruction is bound to continue until not a single house older than this century remains.

CHAPTER SEVEN

Literary Mayfair

NO ONE writes Mayfair novels any longer. Michael Arlen was one of the last of a long line, though even when he was writing his best-sellers in the nineteen-twenties, Mayfair was breaking up, and the great houses such as Devonshire House, Grosvenor House and Lansdowne House already belonged to the past, while others were being pulled down or converted into shops. In the Mayfair of his day after the first World War Shepherd Market had become a smart place to live in, a Hispano-Suiza, 'as supplied to His Most Catholic Majesty, the King of Spain,' the fashionable car to drive, and green a chic colour for women's hats.

To find the first chronicler of Mayfair life we have to go back to the days of King Charles II when John Evelyn noted important local events in his diary. He saw the beginning of Mayfair. When he was a boy London reached only as far as Air Street on the west, but when he died in 1706, aged 86, the fields north of Piccadilly were covered with houses and streets as far west as Bolton Street; and only two years after his death the first guide book to London that included a description of the new quarter, Hatton's *New View of London*, appeared in the book-shops.

Evelyn visited Berkeley House when Lord Berkeley was in residence there, and he lived to see the 'tenements' built by Lady Berkeley on either side of her house: he knew Clarendon House in its glory, and he watched – with a pang – the demolition gangs pulling down the fine house. Finally he became a Mayfair resident himself, and on July 19th, 1699, he entered in his diary:

> I am now removing my family to a more convenient house in Dover Street, where I have the remains of a lease.

The house – it belonged to his son who had died – stood a few doors

32. DORCHESTER HOUSE. Built by Lewis Vulliamy in 1850, Dorchester House was an Italian Renaissance palace transported to Park Lane. It was demolished to make way for the Dorchester Hotel.

33. REGENCY HOUSES IN PARK LANE. A few of the last bow-fronted Regency houses which survive in Park Lane.

34. AT JOHN MURRAY'S. Famous literary figures used to gather in the drawing room at 50, Albemarle Street, the home of John Murray whose descendants still carry on the publishing business at the same house. Sir Walter Scott is talking to Lord Byron (*right*).

35. THE YELLOW BOOK, the exotic publication of the nineties, was published in Mayfair.

up Dover Street on the east side, near the old Dover Street Tube Station, where there are still some early houses, one of which may well have been Evelyn's though no blue plaque marks the site.[1] Dover Street is now no wider than when he knew it, and he may well have dropped into the Duke of Albermarle public house round the corner in Albemarle Street for a glass of ale; he must certainly often have looked up at the Stafford Street sign, now on view inside. He must have reflected, as he saw the press of coaches and hackney cabs and chairmen in the new streets, that he had known the days when it was all green fields hereabouts, with the Tyburn bubbling down the slopes from Hampstead. He had made his contribution to the new residential district, as he laid out Lord Berkeley's garden, probably harnessing the Tyburn to make the 'pretty piscina' which he mentions in his diary.

It was not long before Mayfair appeared in a novel, one of the greatest in the English language – *Tom Jones*. Though Fielding does not use the term, Mayfair is 'the very good part of town' where Tom and his servant Partridge looked for lodgings. They wanted to be near the 'happy mansions' of Grosvenor Square and Hanover Square in their search for Sophia, and they settled down in Bond Street. Whether it was New or Old Bond Street we are not told, but Fielding gives an exact description of the house as if he himself had lived in Bond Street lodgings at some time. As the reader of *Tom Jones* will remember, Tom and his servant lodged at a house kept by Mrs Miller, a clergyman's widow who had been left in straitened circumstances with two daughters, Nancy and Betty. They had little besides their character to recommend them, and also 'a complete set of manuscript sermons', doubtless of the same kind as those which were thundered out from the many pulpits of Mayfair by the Morning and Afternoon Preachers.

Fielding does not tell us what time of year it was when Tom Jones paid his visit to London, but it is not likely to have been May, as in 1749 (the year *Tom Jones* was published) the May Fair was wickedly flourishing and it is not mentioned. An elegant man about town, Mr Nightingale was lodging at Mrs Miller's, occupying the first floor.

I am grown weary of this part of the town, he confided to Tom. I want to be nearer to the places of diversion, so I am going to live in Pall Mall.

So Tom, in his suit of fustian, and his elegant friend left the 'terrestrial

[1] No. 11 according to B. H. Johnson in *Berkeley Square to Bond Street*.

Elysian fields' of Mayfair for Pall Mall in search of amusement. One is tempted to think that had it been May they would not have left Mrs Miller's, as there would have been plenty of diversion near at hand in the fair-ground.

By the middle of the 18th century the street plan of Mayfair was almost completed. In the course of some 75 years the whole expanse of green fields between the Oxford Road and Piccadilly had been covered with houses, except for a small piece of waste land in the north-western corner near the gallows at Tyburn. The rest of Mayfair, as we can see from John Rocque's map, was almost as we know it today and we can use it for following in the footsteps of Mayfair's second most restless literary figure, James Boswell (the other, as we shall see, is Bulwer-Lytton).

Boswell was very much a Mayfair man – attracted by the fashionable houses and the many places of worship there. It is interesting to note that on the day after he arrived in London, on Sunday, November 21st, 1762, he left his lodgings in Pall Mall and crossed Piccadilly to the Mayfair Chapel where he heard prayers and an excellent sermon from the Book of Job on the comforts of piety. Dr Keith had been dead four years, and the tide of Fleet Marriages, now illegal, had dried up, but the Chapel had achieved a tremendous notoriety, and obviously Boswell, being inordinately curious, decided to attend morning service there at the first opportunity to see Dr Keith's famous chapel for himself.

He was often in this neighbourhood as his Ayrshire neighbour, the Earl of Eglinton, lived in Queen Street, and on the following Thursday he crossed into Mayfair again and called on his friend, and dined with him the next day too. So began Boswell's introduction 'into the circles of the great, the gay and the ingenious' in the capital.

He very often attended the public hangings at Tyburn, though he was so distressed by his first experience of an execution that he made straight for Queen Street and asked his friend to relieve his melancholy. It was May 4th, 1763. Can it be that the May Fair had already been closed down? Lord Coventry, whose complaints about the noise put a stop to it, did not move into his new house until the following year, but it looks as if the ban had already come into effect. It is only negative evidence, but Boswell would surely have described the fair in his *Journal* had it been in full swing – and he makes no mention of it.

His distress at the hangings lasted several days, and when he attended divine service at the Grosvenor Chapel on the following Sunday he was unable to concentrate and left before it was over, stepping into a 'Romish Chapel' which filled him with the most 'romantic ideas'. This was the Portuguese Embassy chapel in South Street, since vanished. He was also unable to fix his ideas one Sunday later when he was at morning service at St George's, but this time a member of the aristocratic congregation was responsible for his inattention, the Duchess of Grafton, who 'attracted my eyes too much', he writes in his *Journal*. He was soon living in Mayfair, but always on the move – first in Half Moon Street in 1768, then in Old Bond Street, then Conduit Street and finally Piccadilly, announcing his new address each time in the newspapers.

It was in the Old Bond Street lodgings that he gave his memorable dinner party for Johnson, Goldsmith, Garrick, Reynolds and other friends on October 16th, 1769, at which Goldsmith bragged about his bloom-coloured coat, which Johnson thought so absurd. General Paoli, on whom Boswell danced attendance, lived in Bond Street too.

We do not know where Boswell gave his famous dinner party, as Bond Street was not numbered at this date and the houses were still known by the name of the owner. For instance Bennet Langton, Dr Johnson's friend, lived 'at Mr Rothwell's perfumery in New Bond Street'. Bond Street, both Old and New, was by now almost entirely a street of shops and lodgings. It had become too busy and noisy for private residents, as we know from Gibbon's complaints about the coaches rattling in the street below, and the 'nobility and gentry', for whom Bond Street had originally been built, had almost all moved out. Its history as a residential street hardly lasted for more than a century, but it continued to be in favour with visitors to London, and since there were no hotels in Mayfair at this date, the owners of Bond Street lodgings easily let their rooms as it was an extremely modish address.

Whereas Bond Street lodgings belong to the past, Half Moon Street, where Boswell lived, continued until quite recently to be a street of lodgings or, rather, apartments. In fact there may still be houses with apartments to let such as Somerset Maugham describes in *Cakes and Ale*, published in 1930.

> I walked up Half Moon Street. After the gay tumult of Piccadilly it had a pleasant silence. It was sedate and respectable. Most of the houses let apartments, but this was not advertised by the vulgarity of a card; some had a brightly polished brass plate, like a doctor's, to announce the fact and others the word *Apartments* neatly painted on the fanlight.

One or two with an added discretion merely gave the name of the proprietor so that if you were ignorant you might have thought it a tailor's or a money lender's. . . . My own Miss Fellows had been cook in some very good places, but you would never have guessed it had you seen her walking along to do her shopping in Shepherd's Market.

When Boswell was lodging in Half Moon Street – in 1768 – the Half Moon public house, which gave its name to the street, stood at the western corner facing the Green Park.

Laurence Sterne, the author of *Tristram Shandy*, lived 'over the silk bag shop' in Old Bond Street, later a cheesemonger's, thought to be now the site of Agnew's Gallery. He came to London to launch his *Sentimental Journey* on the Town, but he fell ill in his lodgings. A party of his friends were sitting in John Crauford's rooms not far away in Clifford Street, among them the Dukes of Grafton and Roxburghe, Garrick and Hume, and knowing that Sterne was ill they sent over a footman to enquire after his health. The footman, John Macdonald, later on wrote some curious memoirs in which he described his visit to Sterne.

> I went to Mr Sterne's lodgings; the mistress opened the door. I enquired how he did. She told me to go up to the nurse. I went into the room and he was just a-dying. I waited ten minutes, but in five he said 'Now it is come'. He put up his hand as if to stop a blow and died in a minute.

In these few laconic words written by a footman we are witnesses of the last moments of the author of *Tristram Shandy* and *The Sentimental Journey*.

The witty Sterne was buried in St George's new burial ground near Tyburn, which had been opened a few years before, after the burial ground between Mount Street and South Street had been filled up – due largely, it is said, to the inept work of the surgeons of St George's Hospital. His tomb can still be seen by the wall on the west side, under a tall plane tree. It bears two inscriptions. This is the earlier:

Alas, Poor Yorick.
Near this place lyes
The body of the Reverend
Laurence Sterne
dyed September 13 1768
aged 53 years
Ah! Molliter ossa quiescant.

The inscription contains a curious inaccuracy, as Sterne died on March 18th, and not September 13th, and to correct the error a second grave stone was set up many years afterwards.

To the memory of the Reverend
Laurence Sterne M.A.
Rector of Coxwold Yorkshire
born November 24th 1713
died March 18th 1768
Requiescat in Pace.

This must be the only grave with two epitaphs each giving a different date of death. Both express the pious hope that he may rest in peace. But does he? Resurrection men are said to have snatched his body two days after burial – the deserted Tyburn burial ground was a favourite haunt of theirs – and then sold it to a professor of anatomy at Cambridge, Charles Collignon of Trinity. The Professor unwittingly invited some amateur anatomists to see him operate on a 'subject' recently arrived from London, and it so happened that one of Sterne's friends came into the room during the demonstration and, seeing his partly dissected features, fainted away. It is even said that Sterne's skeleton was kept at Cambridge. There is no record of it being replaced in the grave in Bayswater. Perhaps it is kept at Cambridge still? Should the old burial ground be built over – as seems likely – Sterne's two gravestones would most probably be removed to his Yorkshire parish of Coxwold. When the time comes it will be extremely interesting to see if the grave is empty or not. If the skeleton did prove to be in Cambridge it could then be given decent burial at last.

Towards the end of his life Dr Johnson lived for a short while in Grosvenor Square, where his rich friends the Thrales took Lord Tanker-ville's house, later No. 37, for a few months early in 1781. They set aside a room for him here though it is doubtful whether the Doctor made much use of it, as according to Hannah More 'Grosvenor Square was not half as convenient for him as Bolt Court'. The Thrales lived only a few doors away from a house which had bitter memories for Dr Johnson, where as a struggling young writer he had called on Lord Chesterfield to enlist his patronage for his *Dictionary* and been turned away from the door. He could not forget the slight, whether imaginary or not, and when seven years later his Dictionary was at last coming out and Lord Chester-field 'fell a-scribbling in The World about it', he wrote him a letter 'expressed in civil terms, but such as would show him that he did not mind what he said or wrote, and that I had done with him.' – an under-statement for about the most scathing letter ever written in the English language.

The historical artist, E. M. Ward, painted the scene of Dr Johnson waiting on Lord Chesterfield – a famous picture in Victorian days – but omitted to consult his dates as he shows Dr Johnson sitting impatiently in the sumptuous surroundings of Chesterfield House, while in 1748, when Dr Johnson called on him, Lord Chesterfield had not moved into his new house facing the Park – it was not built until 1750, and he was still living at 45, Grosvenor Square. So we must imagine Dr Johnson fuming with rage at the noble earl in simpler surroundings, sitting in the hall of a house identical with its neighbours Nos. 43 and 44, but we can be grateful to Ward, for obviously he was given permission to set up his easel in Chesterfield House and being a conscientious painter he gives a faithful rendering of the famous staircase and hall of the mansion, now no more.

Johnson once had his pocket picked in Grosvenor Square and John Thomas Smith, Keeper of Prints and Drawings at the British Museum, has put on record in his *Book for a Rainy Day* how the Doctor dealt with him: he seized the thief by the collar with both hands, shook him violently after which he quickly let him loose and then gave him such a powerful slap on the face that he sent him staggering off the pavement. Londoners are not the men they were.

The 19th century now breaks over us, and a tide of writers – novelists, playwrights, diarists, journalists – sweeps over Mayfair. It will be impos-sible to mention more than a few. Byron, the most famous of them all, had two homes in Mayfair – his chambers in Albany, where he lived for only a few months in the early part of 1814, on the left-hand side in the Mansion, taking fencing lessons from Angelo, and looked after by his factotum, old, withered Mrs Mule. It was here that he wrote the *Ode on the Fallen Napoleon*; and after his marriage – since Albany was intended only for bachelors – he settled at 13, Piccadilly Terrace, where he wrote *The Siege of Corinth*. His only child, Augusta, was born here in December, 1815. The house is now numbered 139, Piccadilly and has been refaced, but bears no plaque.

We feel Byron's presence more closely in Albemarle Street, the home of his friend and publisher, John Murray II, whose name 'Mr Murray' is so elegantly engraved on the brass plate of the inner swing door of

No. 50 – a house which so often admitted Byron – and it is occupied by John Murray, the publishers, still.

On March 1st, 1812, Byron woke to find himself famous as the author of *Childe Harold*, a poem which had been refused by 'half the craft' in London. However, an imaginative young publisher, John Murray, who had started up the *Quarterly Review* as an answer to the *Edinburgh Review* with Walter Scott as a contributor, was attracted by Byron's 'oriental poem' and published it. In those days Murray had his offices at 32, Fleet Street, not far from the headquarters of the publishing trade in Paternoster Row. The success of *Childe Harold* floated him westwards, and hearing that a fine house in Albemarle Street was for sale he bought it and established himself there, using it as his home and office. He was the first publisher to leave the traditional home of the publishing trade in the City, settling in a street which was becoming well known for its hotels. Grillion's was nearly opposite at No. 7, Albemarle Street, and Grove's Hotel next door.

No. 50, Albemarle Street soon became the meeting place of the great literary figures of the day. At a time when clubs were not numerous and none was devoted to literature, John Murray's literary friends – Isaac d'Israeli, Sir Walter Scott, Byron, Croker – grew into the habit of calling at No. 50 to chat in his drawing room on the first floor, a large high-ceilinged room with long sash windows looking down into the street. His friends usually called in the afternoon and were known in Byron's words as 'Mr Murray's four o'clock visitors'. According to Jesse, Byron composed the greater part of *The Corsair* while he was walking up and down Albemarle Street. Scott describes in a letter to Thomas Moore his meetings with Byron at this time:

> We met for an hour or two almost daily in Mr Murray's drawing room, and found a great deal to say to each other. . . . I saw Lord Byron for the last time in 1815 after I returned from France. He dined or lunched with me at Long's in Bond Street. I never saw him so full of gayety or good humour to which the presence of Mr Matthews, the comedian, added not a little.

In John Murray II's time No. 49, Grove's Hotel, was taken over as business expanded, leaving No. 50 entirely to the family, and it only ceased to be a private residence on the death of John Murray IV in 1928. Sir John Murray, the present head of the firm and the fifth John Murray in direct line of succession, works in the first floor drawing room, where

John Murray II used to receive his guests, sitting at a large desk at the side of the fireplace.

The fireplace must be mentioned as it was in the grate that Byron's friends, Colonel Doyle and Wilmot Horton, with John Murray II and John Hobhouse standing beside them, burned the manuscript of Byron's autobiography, thus causing his many biographers endless speculation ever afterwards. What secrets went up in smoke on that occasion, and what a best-seller John Murray lost!

Many Byron admirers ask to inspect the famous house, and a recent visitor – from the United States – threw her arms round the bust of Byron which stands on the stairs and left the imprint of her lips, two blodges of red, on Byron's pallid cheeks.

Two of the most prolific of novelists, Bulwer-Lytton and Disraeli, lived in Mayfair for the greater part of their lives, Bulwer-Lytton everywhere and Disraeli at Grosvenor Gate.

Lord Lytton, Baron Lytton of Knebworth, to give him his full title, starts his Mayfair life as plain Mr Edward Bulwer, living in Hertford Street off Park Lane, with his temperamental, almost demented wife, Rosina. Between fits of terrible quarrels he managed to write several novels in Hertford Street, including his best-seller *Pelham*, before setting off for Naples which gave him the material for *The Last Days of Pompeii*. His marriage continued to erupt like Vesuvius and he did not find peace and quiet until on his return to London he rid himself of his wife and set up a separate establishment in the peaceful chambers of Albany. Though even here his wife caused a fearful scene by forcing her way into this bachelor sanctuary. In Albany he was back in Mayfair where he spent most of his London life, but never at one address very long, moving from Albany first to 8, Charles Street off Berkeley Square close to the public house called 'I am the only Running Footman'.

With his fame established as the author of *The Last Days of Pompeii* Bulwer-Lytton set about living up to his reputation, and had the drawing room in his house in Charles Street furnished as the replica of a chamber he had seen at Pompeii, with vases, candelabra, chairs, tables, all in the Roman style, and a perfume pastille shaped like Vesuvius which, when he lighted the cone, sent up a plume of heavily scented smoke. But Bulwer only stayed in Charles Street for two years (1837–1839) and on leaving it began his zig-zag wanderings over Mayfair. We find him at 1, Park Lane a few years later, and Dr Charles J. B. Williams in his *Recollections* describes a visit to Bulwer, who was one of his patients:

When I visited him at his residence in Park Lane even on entrance at the outer door, I began to find myself in an atmosphere of perfume or rather of perfume mixed with tobacco fumes. On proceeding further through a long corridor and anteroom the fumes waxed stronger and on entrance to the presence chamber on a divan at the further end, through a haze of smoke loomed his lordship's figure, wrapt in an Oriental dressing gown with a coloured fez and half reclined upon the ottoman.

In all Bulwer had eleven different addresses in Mayfair, finally settling at 12, Grosvenor Square, and it was from here that his funeral procession started out for his burial in Westminster Abbey on January 25th, 1873.

Dying in the fullness of his fame, both as a politician and a novelist, a movement was started after his death to rename Charles Street after him by calling it Lytton Street. The idea was not well received by the residents. One cannot help thinking that the idea was not so much to honour Bulwer-Lytton as to end confusion by choosing a new name for Charles Street; there was another Charles Street literally within two hundred yards, Charles Street, Grosvenor Square, and one or other of them had to be renamed. (Charles Street was one of the most common street names in London at this time, the total in the post office directory of 1876 amounting to 40.) Luckily Charles Street, Berkeley Square was not changed, largely due to a movement of revolt started by Lady Dorothy Nevill, a great political hostess of the day, and friend of Lord Beaconsfield, who lived in Charles Street nearly all her life. Historically it was right that this Charles Street should retain its name, as it commemorates one of the Berkeley family who used to own the land, Charles Berkeley, Earl of Falmouth. The problem of Mayfair's two Charles Streets was resolved later, however, when the other Charles Street, between Grosvenor Square and Mount Street, was changed to Carlos Place in 1886 in honour of Prince Carlos, later King of Portugal, who married Princess Amélie of France in that year.

Disraeli, unlike his contemporary and friend Bulwer, did not keep changing his address in Mayfair. Having married his rich wife he made her house in Grosvenor Gate his home and, cushioned in the happiness of a successful marriage, he wrote, notwithstanding his heavy parliamentary commitments, the novels of his maturity – *Sybil*, *Coningsby*, *Tancred* and *Lothair* – in the peaceful atmosphere of the white house with the green shutters which looks out over the Park. In 1872, on his wife's death, he left Mayfair for 2, Whitehall Gardens, but he returned at the very end of his life, buying the remainder of the lease of 19, Curzon Street with the proceeds – £10,000 – of his last novel, *Endymion*. He came back to Mayfair to die, as Curzon Street was his home for three months only. A friend calling on him during his final illness found him correcting the proof of his last speech in the House of Lords for Hansard: 'I will not go down to history speaking bad grammar,' Lord Beaconsfield – as he had become – told him, as wrapped in rugs he lay propped up on the couch in his sitting room. A few days later, on April 19th, 1881, he was dead. Both this house and No. 2, Grosvenor Gate, where he spent so many happy years, bear a plaque.

In spite of their long residence in Mayfair, neither Bulwer-Lytton nor Disraeli can be called Mayfair novelists. Perhaps they knew the life around them too well to see it objectively and describe its absurdities. Disraeli was engrossed with the political scene – Bulwer with the historical and exotic.

The position of Mayfair chronicler and observer fell to a non-resident, Thackeray, but before the author of *Vanity Fair*, *The Newcomes* and his parody *Lords and Liveries* could tear down the walls of the social fortress and allow readers inside, those walls had to be built up by the fashionable novels of high life written by the sisterhood of the Silver Fork School, the lady novelists who wrote about Mayfair in the first half of the century.

Their high priestess was Mrs Catherine Gore, authoress, song writer, wife and mother of ten children, who wrote over 60 three-volume social novels before she died blind, worn out and poor at the age of 61 in 1861, having lost the fortune she made by her books through the bankruptcy of her trustee, Sir John Dean Paul. Disraeli described this prolific lady novelist as 'a sumptuous personage like a full blown rose', which is just what one would expect her to look like judging by the eloquent and rich style in which she wrote her fashionable novels of high life. She did know aristocratic Mayfair at relatively close quarters as her husband was Captain Charles Arthur Gore of the Blues, and they were married at the church where so many of her heroines were led to the altar rails – St George's, Hanover Square.

Her novels and those of the other writers of the Silver Fork School not only provided entertaining reading for the subscribers to the hundreds of lending libraries up and down the country, but initiated them into the manners and modes of high society. Before the days of etiquette books (they were soon to descend in a deluge on the newly-emerging middle classes of Victorian England) her novels provided a thousand and one details about the fashionable way of life of London's first society, and also served as a shopping guide, as Mrs Gore liberally sprinkles the vapid conversation of her languid heroines with the names of smart shops – and exclusive hotels.

It is the England of the days before the Reform Bill which lives again in Mrs Gore's novels, as she always seems to have the England ruled by territorial magnates with fantastic rent rolls before her eyes when she writes, even long after the old order had passed away. The working and lower classes do not exist for her. The lowest form of life in her *dramatis personae* is a third or fourth footman, and the middle classes and 'Cits' are only grudgingly allowed entrance to her pages. Hers is the closed world of the anonymous poem in four cantos, *May Fair*, published by William Ainsworth in 1827 during his short excursion into the publishing business in Old Bond Street:

> *Dear to my soul art thou, May Fair!*
> *There greatness breathes her native air:*
> *There Fashion in her glory sits:*
> *Sole spot still unprofaned by Cits.*
> *There all the mushroom, trading tribe*
> *In vain would bully or would bribe:*
> *The Rothschilds, Couttses, Goldsmids, Barings*
> *In other spots must have their parings:*
> *We fix your bounds, ye rich and silly,*
> *Along the road by Piccadilly.*
>
> *. . . land of* ponch romaine *and plate,*
> *Of dinners fix'd at half past eight;*
> *Of morning lounge, of midnight rout,*
> *Of debt and dun, of love and gout,*
> *Of drowsy days, of brilliant nights,*
> *Of dangerous eyes, of downright frights,*
> *Of tables where old Sidney[1] shines,*
> *Of ladies famous for their wines. . . .*

One of Mrs Gore's memorable characters, the Duchess of Trimble-town in *Pin Money*, speaks for the high born world of privilege and

---

[1] Sydney Smith, 'A pleasant creature as lives; but now growing pursy and polemical to a painful degree'. Footnote in original edition (the author was the Rev. George Croly, 1780–1860).

wealth the authoress so excels at describing. The duchess, a stately dowager of the old school, has been told the dreadful secret that a young person whose charms have been the talk of Mayfair ballrooms throughout the season has the terrible misfortune to have been born the daughter of a soap boiler.

'A soap boiler,' cried the Duchess, feeling for her salts. 'I would sooner see every descendant of my house stretched in their graves than disgraced by a commercial alliance. It is the pride of my life that not one of my four daughters was allowed to marry lower than an earldom.'

The Duchess of Trimbletown was probably not quite such a caricature as she seems to be in Mrs Gore's novel. There were many such starchy dowagers presiding over Mayfair's great houses in those days, and a glance at the peerage of the 1820s will show that the daughters of dukes did not make 'commercial alliances', though they soon would.

Mrs Gore's aristocratic characters only spent part of their lives in Mayfair, as they departed for long periods to their country seats, only returning to Town when the leaves of the trees in Grosvenor Square and Berkeley Square were beginning to turn yellow. This was the sign for the blinds, tightly closed all the summer, to be drawn up and for the retinue of retainers – the solemn house-steward, the liveried and powdered footman, the French chef, the housekeeper, the stillroom maid smelling of lemon peel and cinnamon, the sprightly young page and a host of lower servants to prepare for the homecoming of 'My Lord and his Lady' from moor or park, when the London autumn season began; it lasted until Christmas and then again from May to July – a round of balls and routs, assemblies and soirées, and now and then a drawing room or levée when the chosen few were allowed to catch a glimpse of royalty through a haze of bobbing ostrich feathers and diamond headdresses, and perhaps even to kiss the beringed hand of Majesty.

Mayfair had its own language, or rather jargon. Miss Watson, a character in *Arlington*, a novel written in 1832 by Thomas Henry Lister (the only male member of the Silver Fork School), says she is afraid of going to London, because she would not know how to talk to smart people, and when asked how they talk she replies:

Mix a great deal of French with one's English and have the names of singers and dancers and the fashionable shops quite pat. Then one ought to know a great deal of scandal and all about the parties that are going on, and all the marryings that are to be. Then I should be so afraid of getting into disgrace by going where one ought not to go. . . .

Mayfair is only very lightly sketched in by Dickens on his map of London – his taste was not for drawing rooms – and a Dickensian would be hard put to reel off a list of references to it in the novels. Mr Dorrit stayed at a hotel in Brook Street – it could only be Mivart's, later Claridge's – on his return from the Continent where he is visited by Mr Merdle, but there are few other mentions. Dickens knew at least one of its great houses, Devonshire House, as he organised an evening of theatricals there in aid of the ill-fated 'Guild of Literature and Art', acting in a play by Bulwer, *Not so bad as We Seem*, in the Great Ball Room converted into a miniature theatre in the presence of Queen Victoria and the Prince Consort, on May 16th, 1861. Being in his younger days so keen on clothes, he patronised Mayfair's fashionable shops, buying his ties and shirts at a hosiers in New Bond Street, and he had a tailor in Clifford Street. Later in life he often had occasion to go to New Bond Street to Chappells, the music publishers who acted as agents for his public readings. But his closest link with the world of Mayfair was his long friendship with Baroness Burdett-Coutts, the multi-millionaire grand-daughter of Coutts, the banker. The charitable-minded Baroness consulted Dickens on spending the money she gave to good causes; he wrote some 600 letters to her, and they often met to discuss her schemes.

Their usual rendezvous was the Clarendon Hotel in New Bond Street. The Baroness, when she knew Charles Dickens, was unmarried, and perhaps she considered that it would not have been seemly for her to receive him too often at her house in Stratton Street – a cul-de-sac in those days. Here she kept a china cockatoo in the large front bay window overlooking the Green Park to let her friends know whether she was in or out, facing it one way or the other according to a pre-arranged code. The tall brown brick house built by Matthew Brettingham has vanished with the cockatoo (it was Meissen), but no Dickens lover can pass the spot without being eternally grateful that Mrs Brown, a friend of Miss Burdett-Coutts (as she then was), once fell ill in the house. Mrs Brown needed a nurse – it was before the days of Florence Nightingale's nursing reforms – and the garrulous old soul who came came to look after her, with her habit of rubbing her nose along the top of the fender, taking snuff and keeping the bottle on the 'chimley-piece' if she was so 'dis-poged' – as described by Miss Burdett-Coutts and her friend – so fired the imagination of Dickens that he created one of his most extraordinary characters, Mrs Gamp, with her attendant satellite Betsy Prig and the mythical Mrs Harris. Writing to Miss Burdett-Coutts on October 5th, 1846, Dickens told her:

> I do not wish Mrs Brown would be ill again, but I wish she would do something, which would lead to her suggesting another character to me, as serviceable as Mrs Gamp!

When *Martin Chuzzlewit* appeared in book form Dickens dedicated it to Miss Burdett-Coutts 'with the true and earnest regard of the author'. The Baroness has our regard too, for having engaged the prototype of the glorious Mrs Gamp – such an un-Mayfair figure, an importation from Holborn – to look after her sick friend at No. 1, Stratton Street.

Mayfair was not Dickens's world, but it was Thackeray's, with its snobberies and vanities, its cruelties and its grandeur, its plush liveried footmen with their white padded calves taking the air outside the man-sions of Berkeley Square, and its stone-hearted dowagers. The fashionable world of May Fair which Thackeray describes in *Vanity Fair* is the old May Fair of Dr Keith brought up to date, with its noisy booths and puppets, its rogues and worthless characters, its young girls being sold to the highest bidder and its vicious old reprobates who live in its gloomy noble houses; lifting the curtain, Thackeray takes the reader behind the scenes of fashion's citadel for the first time.

Thackeray wrote *Vanity Fair* (and portions of *The Newcomes*) in Kensington, but his knowledge of Mayfair is as thorough as if he had lived there for years. Sometimes he uses the names of existing streets such as Park Lane – Miss Crawley's was one of those white houses with a wide bow-window overlooking the Park – or Curzon Street where Becky lived with her husband 'on nothing a year', or he invents them. His Gaunt Square sets a puzzle for Thackeray lovers, who have never quite decided whether he means Berkeley Square, Hanover Square, or even Cavendish Square outside the boundaries of Mayfair. He was probably thinking of all three. Gaunt House with its 'vast wall' could be Devonshire House or Burlington House, or any of the other great mansions of Mayfair, as at this time they were all shielded from the public gaze by a high wall and all were the scenes of those 'sacred, unapproachable, mysterious, delicious entertainments' which were held at Gaunt House.

It was to one of these entertainments that Becky managed to be invited. Lord Steyne commanded his lady: 'I want you, if you please, to write a card for Colonel and Mrs Crawley'; and much against her will the Marchioness of Steyne, accompanied by Lady Gaunt, 'those severe spotless and beautiful ladies who held the very highest rank in Vanity Fair', had to stifle their pride and drive to Curzon Street and call on the little adventuress.

It is curious how fiction repeats itself. Four decades later in *Lady Windermere's Fan*, Mrs Erlynne installed herself at 84a, Curzon Street, for her onslaught on London society, and one could almost accuse Oscar Wilde of plagiarism in the following passage:

> Lord Windermere: I want you to send her (Mrs Erlynne) an invitation tonight.
> Lady Windermere: You are mad . . . .
> Lord W.: Margaret . . . I insist upon your asking Mrs Erlynne tonight.
> Lady W.: I shall do nothing of the kind.
> Lord W.: You refuse?
> Lady W.: Absolutely.
> Lord W.: Ah Margaret. Do this for my sake. It is her last chance . . . sit down and write the card.
> Lady W.: Nothing in the whole world would induce me.
> Lord W.: Then I will. (Rings electric bell, sits and writes card.)

And a note is sent round to 84a, Curzon Street, inviting 'that woman' to the Windermere's party.

Mayfair – now spelt as one word – had greatly changed since Thackeray's day. The 'Cits', though no one used this rude term any more, had arrived, and 'commercial alliances' were much sought after. In *Lady Windermere's Fan* Lady Agatha Carlisle, with the active encouragement of her mother, the Duchess of Berwick, entered into what the Duchess of Trimbletown would have called a 'commercial alliance' with a Mr James Hopper, an Australian whose father had made a fortune by 'selling some kind of food in circular tins'. We do not know whether they went to live in Australia after their marriage, but it is more probable that the Duchess of Berwick had her way and they bought a house in Grosvenor Square, which 'in spite of there being lots of vulgar people living there', she considered a more healthy place than Australia.

Oscar Wilde wrote *Lady Windermere's Fan* in 1892, midway between the two Jubilees, when England was at the zenith of her power, and

London, the capital of an Empire on which the sun never set, offered a picture of unparalleled wealth and elegance. We see the great ladies of the eighteen-nineties driving in their open carriages with high-stepping horses and two men on the box, along the quiet streets of Mayfair into the Park, their swan-corsetted figures wrapped round with fluttering feather boas, modelling themselves on the exquisite Princess of Wales, and when they walk they even affect the 'Alexandra limp'. On the steps of the clubs stand their menfolk in their elegant frock coats, silk hats, and carrying malacca canes, ready to saunter up Piccadilly, or to climb into a hansom to jingle off to the City where, in the streets near the Bank, men are as elegantly dressed now as in Bond Street.

Sir Richard Grosvenor's estate in Mayfair and the Belgravia estate built by his descendants – with Buckingham Palace between – are society's chosen place of residence. Oscar Wilde's characters reside mostly in Mayfair. The family mansion where Dorian Gray lived in solitary splendour stood in Grosvenor Square near South Audley Street, and the attic, the scene of his macabre end, looked out over the square. His friend, Lord Henry Wotton, lived in Curzon Street, which was also the home of the Duchess of Berwick's nieces, 'the Saville girls', who kept their aunt so well informed about Mrs Erlynne's callers. That 'terrible woman' had taken a house right opposite them, and being always at the window doing their fancy work and making ugly things for the poor, they could not help seeing that Lord Windermere called there four or five times a week.

For a year before his marriage in May, 1884, Wilde lived in Mayfair, in rooms at No. 9, Charles Street (later Carlos Place), kept by a retired butler and his wife – a good vantage point, midway between Grosvenor Square and Berkeley Square, for observing fashionable life.

We move now to Vigo Street – named after Sir George Rooke's victory of 1702 – the narrow lane which juts out of Regent Street and leads past the back entrance of Albany as it broadens into Burlington Gardens. On the south side is the Bodley Head which made literary history in the 'nineties.

John Lane started his publishing business here, putting up the sign – which still distinguishes it – of John Bodley's head. He specialised in beautifully produced limited editions, and the first publication from the Bodley Head was a volume of exquisite poems by an unknown versifier, Richard Le Gallienne. The little bookshop soon became what John Murray's drawing room had been at the beginning of the century – the

36. ASPREY'S IN NEW BOND STREET. Asprey's, the well-known Mayfair jewellers, wisely kept their high Victorian plate-glass shop windows when others modernised their fronts. The doorway on the right led up to Sir Henry Irving's apartments in Grafton Street.

37. REGENCY SHOP-FRONT. Savory and Moore, the well-known chemists in New Bond Street, have kept their Regency shop-front, which is shown as it was before the upper stories were rebuilt. Emma Hamilton bought her medicines here. (Greater London Council)

38. This drawing called 'Peepers in Bond Street, or the Cause of the Lounge' shows how the ladies of fashion, visiting the new shops, had to run the gauntlet of the 'Bond Street Loungers'.

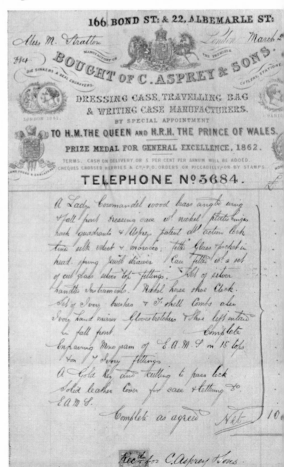

39. EARLY MAYFAIR TELEPHONE NUMBER. Bill for a dressing case supplied by Asprey's of New Bond Street in 1884, when a telephone was an innovation.

centre of literary London, producing that *fin-de-siècle* symbol, *The Yellow Book.*

John Lane had obtained permission from the Trustees of Albany to convert a set of chambers on the ground floor at the end of the Covered Way into his shop, making the bay window of the dining room into the entrance from Vigo Street. Lane used to frequent the Hogarth Club in Dover Street and one evening, talking with Aubrey Beardsley, then an unknown artist aged 22, and Henry Harland, an American, about art and literature, they were challenged by other members of the club to start a really first-class, up-to-date review. Thus was *The Yellow Book* born, with Beardsley as art editor and Henry Harland as literary editor. The first number of the original quarterly appeared in its hard, shocking-yellow covers in 1894 with the Mayfair imprint of 'John Lane, The Bodley Head, Vigo Street'. Many talented writers made their début in its pages. A year later John Lane published the first work of fiction by H. G. Wells in his series called *The Mayfair Set* – a collection of stories called *Conversations with an Uncle.*

The famous Bodley Head premises became well known to bibliophiles for 29 years as Bertram Rota's bookshop. He moved in 1965 to nearby Savile Row, and the house was taken by Sir Allen Lane, publisher of the Penguin Books, where he had started his career 47 years earlier with his uncle, John Lane. Outwardly the famous front with its tall, glass-fronted door, has not changed since the days when many of the rising young literary and artistic figures of the 'nineties called there to see John Lane, the friend of George Moore, Max Beerbohm, Lionel Johnson, Ernest Dowson, Kenneth Graham and Oscar Wilde. Wilde was not a *Yellow Book* contributor, but Lane published his plays and he often called here. Whistler disliked *The Yellow Book*, but he greatly admired the drawing by E. H. New of the Bodley Head shop, which Lane used as the cover of his catalogue. Meeting one day at breakfast at the Hogarth Club, they walked back to Albany together and Lane gave Whistler a copy of the drawing on Japanese vellum.

The Yellow Book would have been in more congenial surroundings in Chelsea, and it ceased publication in 1897. Yet a genuine exotic could flourish in Mayfair. In 1895 a child was born in Roustchouck, a small town on the Danube in Bulgaria, of Armenian parents with the name of Dikran Kouyoumdjian, who made a second home in Mayfair. Changing his name to Michael Arlen he went to an English public school, and as a young man, casting his dark Armenian eyes on the frantic post-war

London, he wrote a series of best-sellers about the cocktail-drinking, nightclub-mad young people of the early nineteen-twenties who lived in Mayfair.

Tall, stern men with their brilliantine-smooth hair parted in the middle, who had been through the hell of war, were his heroes, and physically attractive, wanton 'women of the mode' lightly played the part of *femme fatale*. Most of his books have a Mayfair background, but against this setting he has conjured up a sort of Arabian nights fantasy of romance and love. The author addresses the reader in flowery artificial language which has made his books as dated as the short skirts, plus fours, tasselled cushions, long amber cigarette holders, bobbed hair, co-respondent shoes and cloche hats of the period.

Michael Arlen describes the Mayfair background as he saw it at the moment of writing, so in re-reading *The Green Hat* or *These Charming People* we feel the direct impact of the period of transition when Devonshire House 'was emptily awaiting its destiny, and Lansdowne House held in fief by a distinguished stranger . . .', a delicate way of referring to the tenancy of Gordon Selfridge.

A glossary would be necessary if a new edition of Michael Arlen's novels were published to explain vanished Mayfair landmarks as, for instance, his reference to emptying 'the contents of Solomon's windows' on a grave. Solomon – before the coming of Moyses Stevens – was Mayfair's smart florist and the window, at the corner of Dover Street and Piccadilly, was filled with a wonderful display of flowers, especially carnations and gardenias for men-about-town to wear in their button-holes.

The reason why Lansdowne Passage was open 'on 364 days of the year' would also have to be explained.[1] It was about an incident here that Michael Arlen wrote one of his best short stories, *The Loquacious Lady of Lansdowne Passage.*

> Now one night in May, a year after the world was said to be at peace, George Tarlyon had reason to be walking in a westerly direction from Dover Street: down Hay Hill he went, and down the covered stairway from Berkeley Street into Lansdowne Passage . . . His steps rang gaily between the high walls of the passage, echoes carelessly tossing themselves from one wall to the other, round and about and every way, and he was almost half-way through before he realised

[1] See page 44.

that he was sharing the passage with another, a woman just ahead of him walking, loitering against the wall, a self-effacing woman of the night. . . .

It is a ghost story, therefore doubly suitable for including in this Mayfair anthology, since Lansdowne Passage has also become a ghost of its former self. It was a favourite spot for novelists, and Anthony Trollope used 'the dark uncanny looking passage' as the scene of the murder in *Phineas Redux*. Mrs Gore, too, sent one of her heroes, Danby Ormington, down it, a disgruntled younger son, and she described it as

> that emblem of a younger brother's fortune – mean, dispiriting, and without prospect, with overflowing wealth and enjoyment bounding his views on either side.

Michael Arlen liked this corner of Mayfair, and he gave Berkeley Square its famous nightingale, introducing this mythical bird to the square in his story, *When the Nightingale Sang in Berkeley Square*, in *These Charming People* of 1923.

His story begins:

> There is a tale that is told in London about a nightingale, how it did this and that and, finally, for no apparent reason, rested and sang in Berkeley Square.

He goes on to tell us that the nightingale sang on a night of high drama between a wife, her husband and the wife's lover in a shadowy drawing room of a house 'midway on the entailed side' of Berkeley Square (another note would be necessary here). Its four open windows

> from which the curtains were withdrawn in slack folds of shining silver gave out to the leaves of the trees, which murmured among themselves just a little.

When the drama had been resolved, but to no-one's satisfaction, as it turned out, the nightingale sang:

> A nightingale has never sung before and may never sing again, but if it does it will probably mean something.

– and so the story ends.

But the nightingale did sing again. The dreamy *A Nightingale Sang in Berkeley Square*, first sung in 1940, recalled nostalgic memories of débutante dances of pre-war years. It lasted through the war, though there were no more débutantes, and it is still being played and sung to-day. Berkeley Square would not be the same without its nightingale, and – this would please Michael Arlen – there is a snack bar in Lansdowne Row called 'The Nightingale' and a club in Berkeley Square called 'The Nightingale Club', and thereby – as the author of the *Green Hat* would say – hangs a tale. Mrs Bradman, who keeps 'The Nightingale' in Lansdowne Row, was using the name some time before the nightclub opened. She started her snack bar in 1961, and hung a nightingale in her window; not a live bird – public health regulations would not allow her to keep a live bird, not even a canary where food is being served, and the R.S.P.C.A. would not approve of a nightingale in a cage either. So she has a china nightingale in a china cage. What was her annoyance when, a year or two after she had been serving sandwiches and snacks, cups of tea and coffee to her customers at 'The Nightingale', she saw that a club also called 'The Nightingale' had opened in Berkeley Square. For a while the air over this part of Mayfair was heavy with litigation, but Mrs Bradman, who is a kindly woman with a friendly smile, let the matter drop when, after a change of ownership, the new proprietor of 'The Nightingale' in Berkeley Square agreed to add the word 'club', so now two nightingales sing in Berkeley Square – or rather one in Berkeley Square and the other in Lansdowne Row – in harmony.

CHAPTER EIGHT

Shops Old and New

THE NOBILITY AND GENTRY of Mayfair in the 18th century conducted their shopping at home. The shopkeepers came to the house and after waiting on the hard wooden seats in the hall 'below stairs' (hall seats were always made of wood for fear of fleas, the dreaded plague carriers) they were admitted to the presence of My Lord or My Lady.

Households were also served by street vendors, who wandered through London in their hundreds, entering Mayfair from the crowded, cobbled alleyways of Soho or from the open country and villages to the north, hawking their wares with their plangent cries, a few of which were heard at the beginning of this century. Women in shawls and poke bonnets carried round their fresh milk from a dairy in Queen Street, which had a large golden cow in the window, groundsel sellers stared up at balconies where bird cages hung, dealers in hare and rabbit skins communicated with the cook down in the area of the great houses in Grosvenor Square, and the old clo' man uttered his wail in back streets and mews, and everywhere on wintry evenings the muffin man tinkled his bell:

> My bell I keep ringing
> And walk about merrily singing
> My Muffins!

But their cries are all stilled now.

When Sir Thomas Bond's street was prolonged by New Bond Street as far as the Oxford Road in 1721 (the year when the first houses were rated) the tradesmen saw their chance. Here was a fashionable street cutting through Mayfair from north to south with the 'happy mansions' of Hanover Square and Grosvenor Square on either side, and they either moved into the new houses which were let and sold before they were built, or took over the houses as they were abandoned by the nobility and gentry who found their peace disturbed by the rattling coaches and crowds of loungers sauntering up and down attracted by the new shops and the belles.

The belles in their paint and powder had to run the gauntlet as they were carried in their sedan chairs or rode in their chaises up and down Bond Street. Its narrowness greatly added to its attraction as a lounge, for the belles could be ogled from the very closest range. There was no other street like it in London, and the 'Bond Street Loungers' became well-known London characters, with their own way of walking and wearing their peculiar fashions.

> Let the figure be slender and lounging and slim
> Confoundedly formal and awkwardly trim,
> Hang a hat on his head, let it squint fiercely down
> Or be cut, slashed and scalloped and pared to the crown.
> Behind this strange head, a thick quoif you must tie
> Like a constable's staff or the tail of a lion
> And before, when you try to embellish his hair,
> Befry it and paste it and cut it and curl it
> Now slope it in rangers, in rollers now furl it.
> For the head of a fribble or beau without doubt
> Having nothing within should have something without.
> For a coat give him something so outré in shape
> So awkward, so strange, it would disfigure an ape;
> A thing not a coat, nor a frock, nor a jacket:
> All waist to the bottom, at bottom all pocket. . . .

The Bond Street Loungers paraded in the afternoon at the fashionable hour between two and five. George Colman put them on the stage in his comedy, *The Heir-at-Law*:

> *Lord Duberly:* But why don't you stand up? The boy rolls about like a porpoise in a storm.
> *Dick Dowlass:* That's the fashion, father. That's modern ease. A young fellow now is nothing without the Bond Street roll, a toothpick between his teeth and his knuckles crammed into his coat pocket. Then away you go lounging lazily along.

Bond Street kept its character as a lounge for men until late in the last century – in the eighteen-nineties it was still out of bounds to a young lady especially in the afternoon.

Many shopkeepers leapfrogged into Mayfair from the Strand or the City, like John Brindley, the City bookseller, who gave up his shop near the Pump in Little Britain, and set up business in New Bond Street in 1728, one of the earliest, if not the first, shopkeeper in the famous street. The accession of King George II in the previous year seems to have acted as a stimulus to business in Mayfair, and the enterprising bookseller, being a printer as well, dedicated his first book, *Observations on the Small Pox*, to Queen Caroline, and announced on his trade card emblazoned with the royal arms that he was 'Bookbinder to Her Majesty and the Prince of Wales'. Some of Alexander Pope's poems were published by Brindley, and Horace Walpole bought his books there.

His shop survived for two centuries on its original site at 29, New Bond Street with its double bow window lined with books just as he built it, ending its career as Ellis's – 'The Oldest London Bookshop' – in 1931. This was the bookshop owned by James Robson, who combined piety with business and rebuilt Trinity Chapel in Conduit Street round the corner, and was buried in the Grosvenor Chapel.

Bond Street – Old and New – has not greatly changed its shape since Ralph wrote in 1737 of 'its prodigious length'. He does not mention its narrowness as it would not have struck him in any way extraordinary as the Strand was not much wider. Bond Street is at its narrowest in the 'Bond Street Straits', that gulley-like passage opposite Asprey's at the lower end of New Bond Street with room for not more than two lines of traffic. The 'Straits' have been Bond Street's – and Mayfair's – salvation as they have always limited the amount of traffic Bond Street can take, even since the unfortunate introduction of one-way traffic. Had Bond Street been widened and straightened it would have meant the piercing and quartering of Mayfair – as happened to Soho – which would have sounded its doom as a town within London. Luckily the laying-out of Nash's Regent Street as a north-south artery diverted the attention of the planners from Bond Street for over a century, and the street still pursues its narrow, slightly crooked course through Mayfair with the dip in the middle which Ralph and the Bond Street Loungers knew more than 200 years ago.

Only very few of the houses of those days remain. Here and there one sees examples of 18th-century brick work above the shop level between Victorian and 20th-century reconstructions. The old shop fronts are still rarer, the finest example being Savory and Moore's, the chemists of 143, New Bond Street, which still has its original multi-paned windows on either side of the ornate, canopied porch under the magnificent escutcheon bearing the royal arms, probably the work of the fashionable Regency decorator, George Maddox (1760–1843). Savory and Moore's royal warrant dates back to the days of King William IV. Thomas Field Savory, the first of the family to enter the firm, was a Gentleman of the Privy Chamber of the King, for besides being a clever apothecary he had great social gifts and entertained on a grand scale in the rooms above the shop, giving large dinners to the doctors of the neighbourhood, at which champagne flowed freely.

The Duke of Sussex was one of Savory's friends, and his bulky form used to squeeze through the side door leading in those days up to the private part of the house. The Duke also visited Savory at his house in Sussex Place, Regents Park – they used to play the fiddle together – and after one dinner party his royal guest left with a finely chased silver gilt tankard. The Duke had greatly admired it at dinner, and Savory in an impetuous moment of generosity put the tankard in the Duke's carriage as he drove away. He regretted it afterwards. The Duke, very pleased with his new possession, lost no time in having it engraved with his crest – a lion over a ducal coronet – to leave no doubt as to its ownership. But the Savory family retrieved it in the end. At the Duke's death his possessions had to be put up to auction to pay off part of his enormous debts and it was bought back for £50, its value greatly increased by the addition of the royal arms.[1]

The Savory family also owns a silver cup given to Thomas Savory by Lady Hamilton 'in token of many kindnesses'. Emma lived a few doors away and bought her medicines and ointments at Savory's; the cup may well have been in settlement of a long-outstanding bill. She signed her Will at No. 150, New Bond Street, on September 4th, 1811.

Tessier's, the silversmiths and jewellers, on the other side of the street, has a handsome late Regency window, and it is the only shop in Bond Street which puts up wooden shutters at night. Lewis Tessier, whose father, of French extraction, was a merchant in the City of London, started business at 32, South Audley Street, and moved to the present

[1] Lot 589 in Christie and Manson's sale, on June 27th, 1843, of the 'truly magnificent collection of ancient and modern silver, silver gilt and gold plate of his late Royal Highness the Duke of Sussex, K.G. – a parcel gilt tankard and cover, the surface chased with cupids and arabesques on gilt ground.' The tankard is at present owned by Lieut.-General Sir Reginald Savory, K.C.I.E., C.B., D.S.O.

shop in the middle of the last century. Besides being a silversmith, he was 'an artist in hair', which does not mean he was a hairdresser. He followed a craft, much practised in Victorian days when families were so large, of pressing locks of hair into fern-like patterns under glass, with perhaps the curls of every member of a large family named and dated in one frame. Several of these 'hair pictures' framed in maple wood hang in the shop above the counter, and were used as samples to show to customers.

Nearly every shop in Bond Street at one time had a front window like Savory and Moore's or Tessier's before the introduction of plate glass, when the old multi-paned glass windows began to disappear. In general the old private houses were converted into shops by the addition of a bow-window one storey high on the street level, while the rest of the house was left intact, the back part used as store-rooms and the upper floors either converted into the home of the shop-keeper or let off as lodgings like 'Mr Rothwell's perfumery' in New Bond Street or Sterne's lodgings 'at the silk bag shop' in Old Bond Street.

A loud groan must have gone up from the worthy Bond Street shop-keepers when a proclamation of 1762 ordered the removal of all hanging signs in the Cities of London and Westminster. Before this date, Bond Street, as it tapered up towards Oxford Street, presented a picturesque sight, its four-storey brick houses lined with bow-windowed shops each sporting its individual sign, rivalling the Strand and Cheapside, London's other two main shopping streets, in their variety. Hodgkinson and Warriner, linen drapers in New Bond Street, carried on business at the Turk's Head and Plume of Feathers; John Hilman, cutler of New Bond Street, at the Flaming Sword; Richard Warner, an Italian ware-houseman, at the Two Civet Cats and Olive Tree; James Stephen, a mercer who had moved from St Clement Danes in the Strand, set up his new shop at the sign of the Three Crowns; and Bicknells, James and Griffith, hosiers, where Scott's is today at the corner of Old Bond Street and Piccadilly, at the King's Arms.

All the signs had to be dismantled, being thought dangerous in a high wind, and prosaic numbers took their place; New Bond Street and Old Bond Street each receiving a separate set of numbers which they keep to this day. Old Bond Street, which is still only 200 yards long and 42 yards wide, as it was when Sir Thomas Bond laid it out, is numbered from 1 to 24 on the eastern side as far as Burlington Gardens, and then down again on the opposite side from Benson's at 25, Old Bond Street to No. 50 at the Piccadilly corner. New Bond Street follows the same system: on the eastern side from 1 to 86 to the corner of Oxford Street and down again on the western side to No. 180, where Boucheron's adjoins Benson's. Piccadilly, too, used to be numbered as two separate streets, Piccadilly East and Piccadilly West. It is a sign of individuality that the two Bond Streets have kept their separate numbering to this day. An attempt was made to number them as one street after the first World War, but it met with a howl of protests, especially from Old Bond Street.

Running parallel with Old Bond Street, and almost exactly the same length, is the Burlington Arcade, which has been in its time a lounge for Regency bucks and beaux, a promenade for Victorian swells in their fur-collared coats and dangling their gold-knobbed canes who came to inspect the photographs of 'Professional Beauties' in the shop windows, hoping to meet live ones, too; and, nearer our day, the resort of monocled Edwardian toffs, like 'Gilbert the Filbert, the Knut with a K, the Pride of Piccadilly, the *blasé roué*' – not to mention 'Burlington Bertie', who rose at ten-thirty.

Music hall songs galore celebrated its attractions, but now there are no 'professional beauties' of any kind to be seen in the arcade. All transactions are limited to selling the highest quality goods to the most discerning of customers. Hosiers and jewellers are in the majority, but other shops include a boot-maker's, two bag shops, a tailor and an antique silver dealer. Women and men are about equally catered for. Beadles are on duty to enforce the rules which forbid whistling, singing, playing a musical instrument, carrying a bulky package or an open umbrella, or running. Perambulators used to be banned, but a baby-carriage may now enter. Punctually at 5.30 every evening the commissionaire rings the old brass hand-bell and the arcade is locked for the night. In 1880 it remained open until 8 o'clock, and many an innocent-looking bonnet shop was put to more profitable use after closing hours – the shop keepers used to live upstairs and some had quite commodious living quarters, as we can see from the rows of windows under the vaulted glass roof. Now only cats prowl down its length at night. Its west side is in the parish of St George's, and the east in St James's.

The *Gentleman's Magazine* stated that the arcade was built by Lord George Cavendish, the owner of Burlington House, to stop the annoyance caused him by people throwing oyster shells over his garden wall. But he was more probably given the idea of building an arcade by the many bazaars which were proving so popular in London, like the new Western Exchange almost on his doorstep half way up Old Bond Street. The

Burlington Arcade cost £30,000 and prospered from the start, and it later passed to Lord Chesham, a grandson of Lord George Cavendish. It remained in the Chesham family until 1926 and bears the Chesham coat of arms at either end, with the Cavendish motto 'Cavendo Tutus'. The late Lord Chesham served in the 10th Royal Hussars during the first war, and he recruited the beadles from his old regiment, a tradition still kept up by its present owners, the Prudential Assurance Company. Ask one of the beadles standing on guard at either end, and he will almost certainly reply that he is an ex-N.C.O. of the 10th Hussars.

Mayfair has another arcade as splendidly Victorian as the Burlington Arcade is Georgian, the Royal Arcade linking Albemarle Street with Old Bond Street. Opened in 1879, the Royal Arcade is lined with imposing plate glass shop fronts decorated in black and gold, and we can catch the air of excitement which the Victorians must have felt as they alighted from their carriages in the murky, muddy street outside and strolled down the brilliantly gas-lit, glass-fronted aisle under the soaring roof, accompanied by flocks of children.

Queen Victoria patronised the Royal Arcade, and bought her riding shirts and vests there from H. W. Brettell, hosier and shirtmaker, who used to receive letters from Loehlein, the Prince Consort's former valet. He acted as the Queen's unofficial 'Master of the Robes' and wrote on her heavily black-edged notepaper of which the following letter is a specimen

Osborne, April 18th, 1881

Dear Sir,
Please send me for Her Majesty's account 6 men's undershirts with short sleeves like the last and also some of the same material for ladies and medium size, also with short sleeves.

I remain yours truly,
R. Loehlein.

The Queen bought her shirts at a man's shop because no women's shops cut out shirts in those days. She also bought large-sized men's handkerchiefs of the finest cambric linen at Brettell's and he supplied her with knitting wool which he ordered from Scotland. It was a result of the Queen's patronage of Brettell's and Goodyear's, the fashionable Mayfair florist, now next to Claridge's, that The Arcade (the original name is still carved over the entrance) was renamed the Royal Arcade. (Goodyear's, the royal florist, provided most of the wreaths for King

Edward VII's funeral when the arcade was almost blocked with flowers.)

Brettell's had only two owners for over 80 years. H. W. Brettell moved into the arcade the year after it was built, paying £130 rent, and his son, George Brettell, did not retire until 1964, having joined the firm in 1906 as a boy of fifteen. So it was in the ownership of father and son for over eighty years. When George Brettell joined his father, a stiff dress shirt cost 10s. 6d., all shirts were white and the first man to wear a striped shirt and striped collar in about 1910 was 'rather a dog'. Silk stocks and stand-up Fitzwilliam collars were still worn, but the wing collar was the latest style. During his fifty-nine years in the Royal Arcade George Brettell reckons he cut out over 10,000 shirts, and he always wielded the 18-inch shears used by his father for cutting out Queen Victoria's shirts. Like his father, he had many royal customers, among them 'Prince George' and 'Prince Henry', as he still called the late Duke of Kent and the Duke of Gloucester up to the time of his retirement.

The Ballad of Reading Gaol, by C.33, made its first appearance in the Royal Arcade. Leonard Smithers, the rather shady publisher, had his shop at Nos. 4 and 5, Royal Arcade, directly opposite Brettell's, and Oscar Wilde's celebrated poem was published here in 1898 and sold at 2s. 6d. a copy. Leonard Smithers soon afterwards moved to 5, Old Bond Street.

Mayfair's oldest shop was in Berkeley Square. Known to generations of Londoners, and visitors, for its delicious ices and ball suppers, this was the famous confectioners, Gunter's. Before the east side of Berkeley Square was rebuilt Gunter's used to be at No. 7, four doors away from Horace Walpole's house, and Walpole certainly knew it. It was founded in 1757 by an Italian pastrycook, Domenico Negri, who took Gunter into partnership 'making and selling all sorts of English, French and Italian wet and dry sweet meats, Cedrati and Bergamet Chips, and Naples divolini' and other delicacies at the sign of the Pineapple in Berkeley Square (it had no number then). Gunter's was also famous for its turtle soup, made from 'turtles killed in Honduras', and for its many-tiered, elaborately decorated wedding cakes.

The same Mayfair families dealt with Gunter's for many generations, and almost unlimited credit was given. Charles Manners Sutton, the Speaker of the House of Commons, who lived in Berkeley Square, ran up bills for dinners from 1824 to 1828 which amounted to £545. 6s. before he finally paid. The Duke of Sussex probably never settled his bills in his lifetime, as they climbed to £698. 9s. 6d. from 1819 to 1828, with small sums paid on account from time to time after letters written to Mr Stephenson at Kensington Palace.

Nathan Rothschild ran up bills, too, but they were paid regularly. He lived at 108, Piccadilly and, being Austrian Consul-General and head of the Rothschild bank, entertained on a lavish scale. He gave an enormous party – to judge by the items in Gunter's ledger – on July 4th, 1827. Here are some of the prices:

Haunch of Venison	£5.		
33 pounds of grapes	19	16	0
24 champagne at 7/6	9	0	0
2 fine pineapples	3	18	0

The cost of champagne was considerably higher than the usual price for the period, which was 43s. per dozen duty paid; these may have been magnums. The price of pineapples seems excessive to us, but it was before the days of refrigeration ships and pineapples had to be expensively grown in English hothouses. Being such a luxury, the sight of a luscious pineapple on a dinner table was a sure indication of the wealth of the host.

Gunter's also provided a 'man cook' for Nathan Rothschild's party, and eight attendants. He charged five guineas for the cook and one guinea each for the eight attendants, and their names are even entered in the margin of the ledger – one of them to become very famous in the history of Mayfair's hotels: Claridge.

As a sidelight on the old custom of oiling the helping hand there is a note in the ledger that when Rothschild's bill of £562. 7s. 6d. was settled on March 28th, 1828, various tips were handed out: Edwards, presumably the butler, was given £5, James £3 and 'cook' £2.

Gunter's ices were said to be made from some secret recipe. Mrs Gore in one of her novels speaks of an ice from Gunter's quite unknown today, a 'white currant ice'. It was an old-established Mayfair custom that you did not partake of Gunter's ices inside the shop, but under the trees of Berkeley Square on the other side of the road. Here in the summer barouches and fashionable equipages ablaze with escutcheons would be drawn up in the shade of the plane trees, and the ladies seated inside would sip sorbets and eat ices while their attendant gentlemen lounged and lolled by the railings, and waiters dashed to and fro across the square, their trays laden with tinkling glasses.

Now with refrigerators in almost every home and cheap ices brought to the door by a motor van sounding a carillon it is difficult to imagine a time when ices were a rare luxury, as the following announcement in *The Times* of July 5th, 1827, so clearly shows:

> Messrs Gunter respectfully beg to inform the nobility and gentry who honour them with their custom that this day having received one of their cargoes of ice by the *Platoff* from the Greenland Seas they are enabled to supply their cream fruit ices at their former prices.

Bulwer-Lytton, when he lived in Charles Street, would often have joined the group under the trees as he lounged across the square on his way to Bond Street, the 'dear street' of his lines in *The Siamese Twins*:

> *And now our brothers Bond Street enter*
> *Dear Street, of London's charms the centre*
> *Dear Street, where at a certain hour*
> *Men's follies bud forth into flower*
> *Where the gay minor sighs for fashion;*
> *Where majors live that minors cash on*
> *Where each who will may suit his wish,*
> *Here choose a Guido – there his fish.*

Was there really a fishmonger's in Bond Street in Bulwer's day, or did he introduce the word 'fish' for the sake of the rhyme? It is possible to check up if he is joking or not, as a few years later, in 1840, Tallis published his *London Street Views*, and Bond Street, New and Old, is one of the streets included in the collection with every shop faithfully drawn, named and numbered. The nearest approach to a fishmonger's on the east side is Thomas Kirby at 36, New Bond Street, an oilman who sold fish sauce. But sure enough, on the west side two doors before the slit opening into Lancashire Court, at 121, New Bond Street, is Bulwer's fishmonger: 'J. Kenneth, Fishmonger, wholesale and retail', drawn with exactitude, even down to the slab, and further, we can recognize the house as it is one of the few original brown brick Georgian houses to have survived in New Bond Street. Now James Oakes, Antique Dealer, occupies the premises. Surprisingly enough, Bond Street, according to Tallis's views, had two fishmongers at this period, as there is another at 4, Old Bond Street: George Poulton, a Royal Warrant holder. So Bulwer was quite right about the fish; but in his day Bond Street was more of a general shopping street than it is today – Mayfair's high street, in fact, its many kinds of shops serving the needs of the residents, and because they sold such high-quality goods they nearly all enjoyed the patronage of the Royal family – a tradition still maintained.

As for buying one's Guido, Bond Street had its art galleries then as now, but Sotheby's, the famous auctioneers, in Bulwer's day was still in Wellington Street, Covent Garden, and it did not come to New Bond Street until the first World War when it moved to the chapel-like Doré Gallery on the east side renowned for its religious pictures in the last century. Sotheby's brought its talisman with it, the black basalt bust of Sikhet, the lion-headed goddess of Egypt, which used to guard the approach to the old sale room in Wellington Street and now looks out at New Bond Street over its ecclesiastical entrance.

Television cameras have made Sotheby's auction rooms upstairs familiar to millions of viewers, but less well known are the vaults below street level receiving a never-ending stream of books, pictures, furniture, porcelain, arms, armour, and every variety of *objet d'art* which are stored here before they are neatly classified in lots inside the covers of Sotheby's famous green catalogue, described perhaps as 'The Property of a Lady of Title'. The vaults used to be the cellars of the Black Horse Inn, and they stretch from New Bond Street almost to St George's Church.

Works of art are also sometimes stolen from Mayfair, and the drain has been continuing since the day when Princess Anne's silver cistern disappeared from Berkeley House. Of all the robberies committed in Mayfair the most sensational – because so many years elapsed before it was recovered – was the theft of Gainsborough's famous portrait of Georgiana, Duchess of Devonshire, which was stolen from Agnew's galleries in Old Bond Street ninety years ago.

Sir William Agnew, son of Thomas Agnew, the founder of the firm, bought Gainsborough's famous portrait of the Duchess wearing a large Leghorn hat, at the Wynn-Ellis sale at Christie's on May 6th, 1876, paying the enormous sum of 11,000 guineas for it, a price which attracted a great deal of attention. A certain Adam Wirth, alias Henry Raymond, had noticed the high price, too. Visiting the galleries late one afternoon he hid in the shop just before closing time and when the staff had left he cut the picture out of its frame, rolled it up and passed it through the window over the main entrance to two accomplices waiting below. A policeman happened to pass at the critical moment, but the nimble Wirth stepped back into the window until the danger passed.

Away the picture was rushed to St John's Wood, where the thieves kept it under a mattress. To sell such a well-known picture was impossible, but the thieves thought that Agnew's might be induced to part with a large sum for its return, and a series of ill-written letters signed 'New York' reached Sir William threatening to destroy the picture unless . . . and to prove they had the 'Dutchess' in their possession the thieves cut off bits of the canvas and enclosed them in their letters. Sir William Agnew replied, as instructed, through the personal column of *The Times*, but he refused to compound a felony.

One argument the thieves used was that, in paying up, Agnew's would more than recoup themselves by the price the 'noble lady' would fetch – a certain delicacy prevented them from calling the picture by its full name – following the enormous interest the theft had aroused. But Sir William still refused to be held up to ransom.

Years passed, and then in 1901 – the picture by now having crossed the Atlantic – the last survivor of the gang communicated with Pinkerton's National Detective Agency in Chicago, asking them if they would be prepared to act as a go-between to restore the picture to Agnew's – for a consideration, of course.

Sir William by this time had retired, and his son, Morland Agnew, after taking advice from Scotland Yard, undertook to represent the firm and set out for the Middle West. The two parties never set eyes on one another, as the deal – the most astonishing in the history of picture transactions – took place in a suite of rooms with communicating doors in a Chicago hotel, Pinkerton's detectives in the central room and Morland Agnew and the last representative of the gang of thieves on either side; the picture was passed from one room to the other. The price that was paid to retrieve it has never been disclosed.

The return of Morland Agnew with the 'Noble Lady' was like a triumphal progress – ballads and sensational articles appeared in the papers, and the picture even inspired the writer of a popular song, *The Stolen Duchess*. It was then put on sale and crossed the Atlantic once more to enter the collection of the American millionaire, John Pierpont Morgan. This price, too, is a secret, but Duveen believed it to be £30,000. The Duchess now hangs in the Metropolitan Museum, New York.

Two generations of Agnew's have entered the family firm since those stirring days, and the senior director is Mr Colin Agnew; but the Red Gallery on the first floor from where Adam Wirth stole 'the Dutchess' is still much the same, though the front of the house has been rebuilt. (No. 45,[1] two doors away, is an example of one of the Old Bond Street

[1] Known as Sterne House – see page 116.

40. ROYAL ARCADE. Originally called The Arcade, it was renamed the Royal Arcade after Queen Victoria patronised Brettell's, the hosiers.

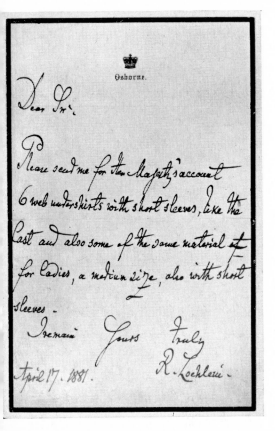

41. ROYAL CUSTOMER. A letter written by R. Loehlein, the Prince Consort's former German valet, to Brettell's, the hosiers, in the Royal Arcade, ordering 'web undershirts' for Queen Victoria.

42. PULTENEY HOTEL. The Czar Alexander of Russia and his sister the Grand Duchess Catherine stayed at the Pulteney Hotel overlooking Green Park on their visit to London in 1814. (Crace Collection, British Museum)

43. BURLINGTON ARCADE. The Burlington Arcade, a favourite lounge for Regency bucks and Victorian gentlemen, gave its name to a waltz which was a popular hit in the 1870s.

houses built by Sir Thomas Bond.) Agnew's business of buying and selling Old Masters goes on the same, though there is a lack of Old Masters; but then there always was. Even Sir William would often lament: 'We are running short of pictures. Whatever shall we do?'

There is one side of their business which has changed, however – the mass sale of prints of famous pictures at two guineas each. The prints used to be stored in their thousands in the basement under the pavement of Old Bond Street. Now the vaults are used for framing and other purposes. It is interesting to go down to the vaults as one can see the very bricks which Sir Thomas Bond must have watched being laid when he built his street on the site of old Albemarle House.

Most of Bond Street's fashionable shops replaced their Victorian plate glass windows after the first World War, just as their predecessors had scrapped their Regency windows. One shop wisely ignored the rage to be modern; Asprey's, the jewellers and silversmiths in New Bond Street, which can boast the finest example of Victorian shop windows in London. They rise to two storeys, supported by tall, slender acanthus-crowned pillars, and are nearly four times as high as the shoppers who look into them.

This old family firm was founded by William Asprey in 1781 in Mitcham, where he had a flourishing business making the new fitted dressing cases which were so fashionable throughout the 19th century. He set up shop at 49, New Bond Street and in 1848 the firm moved to their present address, a four-storey Georgian house in the 'Bond Street Straits'. Soon afterwards Asprey's received the Royal Warrant, which they have held ever since. Under the chairmanship of Mr Philip Asprey, four members of the family take an active part in running the business.

When Princess Ena of Battenberg, Queen Victoria's grandchild, married King Alfonso of Spain in 1906, Asprey's made the dressing case which was presented to her by the residents of the Isle of Wight. The staff at Asprey's have long memories, and Mr Hubbard, who remembered the dressing case being made, having started as a youngster in the shop the previous year, was serving the Queen of Spain some 55 years later, and asked her if she still had it. 'The case has gone, Mr Hubbard,' the Queen replied, 'but the silver fittings are still on my dressing table.'

Many of the goods on display in the brilliantly lit mirror-lined show-rooms – the silver cigarette cases, gold cigar boxes, crocodile-skin bags, and fine leather work – are made on the premises, three storeys up on the top floor of the old building, by the firm's own craftsmen. Mr

Algernon Asprey, of the sixth generation of the family and a Freeman of the Worshipful Company of Goldsmiths, spent a year on the bench there and is now the chief designer. But many of the more expensive and elaborate objects he designs are never seen in the shop. They are flown out to the oil sheiks in the Middle East (who have taken the place of Indian Maharajahs as Bond Street's best customers) or are made to order for customers at home.

Round the corner in Asprey's building, at 22a, Grafton Street, are the rooms where Henry Irving lived, returning here to his solitary existence after his great triumphs at the Lyceum Theatre in the Strand. A very steep staircase leads up to the two floors he occupied, now turned into offices which structurally have remained almost unaltered since his day.

It is now time to remember Mayfair's most famous dog, who must earn a place in any canine valhalla – Tiny, a King Charles spaniel whose bark was often heard in the 'Bond Street Straits' as her master, William Bishop, the Bishop of Bond Street, a rare London character, kept his gun-making shop just near at 178, New Bond Street. The brown brick house still exists, and is now Savory's, the tobacconists.

The Bishop of Bond Street wore a snow-white apron and tall shiny hat. The hat was so much part of him that he was never seen without it, and one day when he was ill a customer rushed upstairs, hoping to surprise him without his famous headgear, but found him wearing his top hat in bed.

All London cabbies knew him and he was such a well-known character that a clergyman was driven to 178, New Bond Street instead of Fulham Palace, as he had failed to make it clear to the cabby that the Bishop of London, not the Bishop of Bond Street, was expecting him to dinner.

Now Tiny comes into the story, as one day she was stolen, and her master went through such agonies of mind thinking of the dreadful fate that might have overtaken his pet that he determined to make dog-stealing a far greater offence in future. Mayfair was one of the chosen haunts of the dog thieves, who carried on a very thriving business. They always carefully chose their dog and, after removing its collar, black-mailed the fond owner into paying a large sum to have the pet returned, or if this did not work they sold the dog to a pair of Frenchmen who carried on a lucrative export business to the continent. Even the Queen's dog, Cherry, also a King Charles spaniel, was stolen and the whole London police force was mobilised to find it, a reward of £100 being offered; Cherry was returned only after a deal had been made in the underworld of dog-stealers.

The Bishop, in support of his campaign, cited the Queen's case and many others who had been held up to ransom, including the Duke of Cambridge who paid £50, and Count d'Orsay and Mr White, Police Magistrate, who each paid £10 to retrieve their pets.

Owing to the Bishop's persistence – he is said to have spent £1,000 on the campaign – his Bill was passed through Parliament and was known as Bishop's Act, and the theft of Tiny was the cause of it all. Happily for her master's peace of mind, his pet was found and lived to the ripe old age of 15, dying on August 25th, 1844, and was buried in the area of the Bishop's shop with this inscription:

Beneath this tablet
are deposited in soldered lead the remains
of a faithful and affectionate
dumb companion
Let not the reader smile at so unusual a tribute
to one of the brute creation
For the fidelity she bore her master exacts from
him this last sad testimony
to his poor dog
whose sagacity, intelligence and
devoted attachment
for fifteen years towards him
who reared and cherished
TINY
would have done honour to a
human being.

On Sculptured stone we mark the hallow'd spot
Where friends are laid who ne'er can be forgot;
Man pays this tribute to departed worth,
When human troubles finish here on earth.
If friendship merits such a record, then
The dog may surely claim the like from men;
Their best companion, ever faithful friend,
True to the last, devoted to the end!

With rich or poor she shared the meat or crust,
To neither was she known to fail in trust!
With sorrowing hand, in these few lines I trace

The merits of the noblest of her race;
Intelligent as faithful, docile as sincere,
(e'en as I write I check the falling tear)
Of beauty rare and instinct unsurpass'd
Such was poor 'Tiny' even to the last!
Farewell, dear friend, as of the grave I view,
A master's tear shall this sad spot bedew.

The Bishop survived his little four-legged friend by many years and when he died in 1871 aged 74 he had the honour of having his obituary published in *The Times*. He left behind him a host of friends with many happy memories of rat hunts, cock fights, a bout with the gloves, or a practice with the duelling pistols in the cellars beneath the old gun shop. He was a vintage cockney character who spent his life in Bond Street. We can see what he looked like as his portrait – wearing his snow-white apron and glossy black hat, and holding a gun, of course – hangs in Mr Malcolm Lyell's office at Holland and Holland, the gunmakers in Bruton Street, with Tiny barking at his feet.

In the golden age of gun-making before 1914 Mayfair could count many gun-makers, four in Bond Street alone, and the most famous of all, Joseph Manton, who had his shop at 313, Oxford Street, near Hanover Square. He went bankrupt in 1826 and James Purdey took over his premises. Purdey's today is in South Audley Street, a gun-shop with a world-wide reputation. James Purdey I was lured into Mayfair by none other than the first Duke of Westminster, who said to him one day, while he was still in Oxford Street: 'Purdey, your business is expanding. I have the ideal site for you,' and he offered him a shop on his land at the corner of Mount Street and South Audley Street. But being a cautious man Purdey reinsured himself when he moved into his new spacious premises. In the 1870s art was booming, and Victorian merchant princes paid high prices for pictures, so he built his new shop with a long gallery lighted from a window in the roof, which could be converted into a picture gallery if gun-making failed. But, of course, with such rich and powerful patrons as the Duke of Westminster, and later the Prince of Wales, his business flourished and the Long Room – as the gallery of Purdey's is called – is lined with pictures of his patrons, and filled with souvenirs of the firm's success.

Four generations of the Purdey family look down from the walls, James Purdey I, the founder of the family's fortunes, in a place of honour over the fireplace, and James Purdey II holding one of his guns. The white glass gas globes and the horse-hair furniture give an air of well-being and masculine comfort – we might be in the billiard room of a large Victorian country house. King Edward VII and the Duke of Cambridge in shaggy tweeds with their ladies in tailor-mades and tweed caps look out from many shooting groups on the walls. The stuffed white pheasant in the window in Mount Street was a present from the King, who shot it when Prince of Wales in 1885. King Alfonso of Spain bought his guns here, and his photographs fill a small room. King George V, too, used to come to the Long Room to order his guns, and among the many souvenirs there is a miniature gun, only $7\frac{1}{2}$ inches long, which is a replica of the pair now at Sandringham presented to King George V by Tom Purdey on the King's Silver Jubilee in 1935. All three models were built by the present managing director of the firm, Mr Harry Lawrence, and they fire miniature cartridges which cost I.C.I. much time and money to make. Tom Purdey, the last member of the family in the business, died in 1957 and the Chair in the Long Room is occupied now by Lord Sherwood.

Many Mayfair firms run in dynasties. Goode's, almost next to the Grosvenor Chapel in South Audley Street, is a family firm. William Goode, 'a chinaman', founded the firm in Mill Street in 1827 behind St George's Church where he was a tax-collector, and when his business prospered he moved west, jumping over Bond Street to South Audley Street, which was Mayfair's second smartest shopping street. He took a plot of land on a 99-year lease (since prolonged) from the Marquess of Westminster in 1845 and built his palatial shop, still one of the most impressive in Mayfair, and the largest china and glass business under one roof in the world. His great-grandson, Mr T. M. Goode, is a director of the firm.

Taxi drivers are often asked by visitors to London to drive to the 'Elephant Shop', and they do not have to ask for any further particulars as they know that Goode's is meant, as in the windows are two richly caparisoned china elephants carrying golden howdahs. They were made by Minton for Messrs Goode, and are as old as the Eiffel Tower as they were shown at the Paris Exhibition of 1889. Ever since, they have stood in Goode's window and are well-known London landmarks, belonging in fact to London's 'Other Zoo'.

One day a little old man was seen standing on the pavement outside the shop intently examining the two elephants in the window which seemed to have a fascination for him. Then, plucking up his courage, he came in through the main door and glancing shyly about him – he did not look a regular customer – he asked to speak to Mr Goode. He had been at Minton's in the eighteen-eighties, he told him, and he remembered the elephants well. When they were sent off to Paris by Pickfords they were packed in a large wooden case and, being the smallest person in the works, he had been lifted inside and told to jump up and down on the straw to ensure they were firmly packed. He had not seen the elephants from that day to this, and of course recognised them immediately when he passed them by chance in the window. His story delighted Mr Goode.

Mount Street, laid out by Sir Richard Grosvenor on the southern fringe of his property, was named after Oliver's Mount thrown up nearby to defend London from the Royalists at the time of the Civil War. It bordered on St George's burial ground, then in full use, and was a seedy street avoided by the quality, not made any more cheerful by the Parish Workhouse, offering its inmates an uninterrupted view of the mouldering graves. The Watch, too, had its headquarters in Mount Street, replaced later by Mayfair's first Police Station when 'Bobbies' were introduced. At the western end near Hyde Park, Mount Street joined Tyburn Lane, and every month or so when there was an execution at Tyburn the whole town used Mount Street as a short cut to the gallows. After the mob had gaped its fill at the horrors they poured down Tyburn Lane and turned into Mount Street on their way back to their rookeries farther east.

When the tombstones were removed in 1888 and the burial ground transformed into a garden, Mount Street's fortunes changed. The plain houses of ten or twelve rooms were pulled down and replaced by finely-built terracotta red apartment blocks designed in the fashionable 'Dutch' style, with chambers for bachelors on the upper floors – the first of their kind in London – and rows of small well-planned shops below. Mount Street, except for a few isolated examples of rebuilding, has hardly changed since those days, when it was one of the most fashionable addresses in London for bachelors, the chambers letting for £500 a year, those on the south side looking over the garden where the graveyard used to be. Mount Street was always very popular with estate agents who are still represented there, but they are not as numerous as they used to be, and now the old-established London bookshop, Bumpus, has opened in Mount Street after hovering on Mayfair's borders for many years.

The firm was founded by John Bumpus about 1790 at St John's Gate,

Clerkenwell: thence he removed in 1814 to Holborn Bars where he was succeeded by his son, Thomas, the friend of Dickens and other writers. The move west was made in 1847 by John Bumpus II, grandson of the founder, who established the House of Bumpus on the famous island site between the branches of Marylebone Lane at 330, Oxford Street, directly opposite Davies Street where the Tyburn flows from Marylebone into Mayfair. The bookshop remained here until demolition forced it out in 1935 when, with the late Mr John Wilson as managing director, it moved farther towards Marble Arch to premises on the south side of Oxford Street, and it now comes into the heart of Mayfair after a short spell in Baker Street.

Mount Street residents, and others who live nearby, have shown their appreciation of the gardens by giving seats which are inscribed with their names. May Adelina Whittaker, 'who so much enjoyed these gardens', has given a seat. Florence Tyzak Bigland, who lived in a flat overlooking the gardens, also wished to be remembered in this way, and Captain C. J. Leslie, M.C., a resident of Mount Street, has given a seat, too. Thanks to these gifts (to the Westminster City Council) we may sit in the garden under the tall plane trees and enjoy its peace and quiet. The thirsty, too, have been remembered and a drinking fountain shaped like a well provides a gush of water at the push of a button – the gift of Henry Lofts, an estate agent 'in recognition of many happy years in Mount Street'. The small copper plate also bears the inscription 'Sir Ernest George R.A. fecit 1892.' Therein lies almost the whole history of the new Mount Street, as Sir Ernest George with his partner Harold Peto built the terracotta red houses and Henry Lofts, the estate agent, let and sold them.

The commercialisation of Mayfair has meant the destruction of its old houses or has made them serve purposes for which they were never fitted. One exception springs to mind: Bourdon House at the southern end of Davies Street where Mount Street joins it. How easily this perfect Georgian house could have been swept away: as an excuse for pulling down the beautiful or the historic can always be found (though it is getting more difficult now). But instead, the old house has been furnished with antiques. Mallett's, the antique dealers of New Bond Street, took Bourdon House on a long lease from the Grosvenor Estate a few years ago, and made it into a show house. A wood fire crackles in the grate, the rooms are carpeted and the furniture is arranged as if visitors were expected and the host or hostess were about to come downstairs. It was one of the first houses built on Sir Richard Grosvenor's estate by William Bourdon and looked across the fields at Hugh May's Berkeley House, its nearest neighbour to the south. It is one of the most charming and delightful houses in London, and has a small courtyard garden shaded by tall plane trees. The Duke of Westminster chose it as his London residence in the first World War when Grosvenor House was turned into a hospital, and it remained his home until his death in 1953.

Mayfair, besides the Burlington and the Royal Arcades, has an open arcade, Lansdowne Row, a walking street lined with small shops leading from Berkeley Street to Fitzmaurice Place. It is really Lansdowne Passage above ground, as it runs parallel to the old right of way which is now shut. With its tubs of flowers, trees and seats, it is one of Mayfair's smallest but most successful new ventures, and its two rows of shops, especially coffee bars, are crowded at the lunch hour.

At No. 22, a few doors away from 'The Nightingale', Mr Mackett Beeson spends his days – and perhaps his nights too – surrounded by his Lilliput population of chessmen . . . chessmen in wood, metal, soapstone, porcelain . . . neatly ranged on their boards: some are of great rarity, like his Meissen set valued at more than a thousand pounds, and at the other end of the scale is the wooden standard Staunton set of 32 pieces costing a pound or two. On an average he keeps a stock of 300 sets of chessmen on shelves all round his shop and in the window. He is the one and only chessman specialist in the world, and has clients in every country waiting anxiously for news that he has found the set they want. One customer in Aden has had a small palace built for her chessmen, with plenty of room for more sets. Collectors of chessmen do not always play chess. Some do not even know the moves. They collect rare and beautiful sets of chessmen for the delight they give the eye, and conversely no serious chess player would ever think of playing the game with any set but the Staunton standard. Mackett Beeson has built up his world wide business in a remarkably short time, starting in 1949, and he is the first of his line with no dynasty behind him; but Agnew's, Asprey's, Goode's and Purdey's, and many other famous Mayfair family firms had to start once.

One of Mayfair's first shops was a bookshop, John Brindley, and Bond Street continued to attract booksellers for nearly two centuries afterwards, until the high rents drove them out. Their hey-day was the first half of the last century when bookshops and lending libraries abounded in Bond Street, the most famous being Mitchell's 'Booksellers and Publishers to

Her Majesty', at the corner of Old Bond Street and Stafford Street where Yardley's new shop is now. The gorgeous Lady Blessington, who lived in one of the white houses overlooking the Park in old Seamore Place,[1] had an account at Mitchell's, and in 1832 she bought 17 volumes of Byron's works. Some of her other purchases are curious: Henderson's *Rules for Health*, 6s.: Burton's *Anatomy of Melancholy*, 24s.: *The Law of Husband and Wife*, 18s.: and she had also to buy several copies of her own works to give to friends, especially her *Book of Beauty* and her *Conversations with Lord Byron*.

D'Orsay, too, patronised Mitchell's, which was a meeting place for Regency bucks, and bought all his drawing materials there – vast quantities of pencils, white drawing paper, drawing pins; and in his role of Bond Street lounger and dandy he was perpetually ordering new supplies of perfumed visiting cards. Mitchell's, like other West End shops, gave unlimited credit, but they were lucky if they ever saw d'Orsay's money unless they took his drawings in exchange, which they were still selling in the 'eighties. Queen Victoria, who seldom entered a shop in London, paid a visit to Mitchell's and a small brass plate let into the doorpost of the old shop commemorated the occasion.

The Bond Street bookshops and lending libraries also dealt in theatre tickets, which was their salvation as they were faced with ruin when Mudie's Lending Library started up in Oxford Street with subscriptions of only one guinea a year. Theatre booking agencies are still known as 'libraries', dating from the time when the small exclusive bookshops and lending libraries in the West End sold boxes and seats at the Opera, the Adelphi, Astleys and other places of amusement.

Heywood Hill's bookshop in Curzon Street links up with the fashionable libraries of Bond Street, as it is not only a place to buy books but a meeting place, at its most crowded before and after luncheon when it is quite difficult to squeeze between the tables piled high with the latest best-sellers. It is the bookshop of the Literary Establishment, authors and especially book reviewers treating it as an annexe of the London Library in St James's Square, scouring its shelves for the rare and the unusual. Nancy Mitford worked at Heywood Hill's during the war when the owner was in the Army. She is said to have scattered her 'Darlings' on customers rather too indiscriminately, and one client was heard to remark testily: 'A few less darlings, and a little more attention, please.' Her witty salesmanship, combined with Trumper's famous hairdressing establish-

[1] Now Curzon Place.

ment next door, its window plastered with royal coats of arms, made this a very special corner of Mayfair, which it still is. Some customers combine visits to both, and new books bought at Heywood Hill's get left at Trumper's and bottles of Trumper's 'perfect dressing for the hair' are often found on the shelves at Heywood Hill's.

Shepherd Market beckons to us a few yards further down Curzon Street, through the archways on the left. Approach it this way or down 'the dark cavernous artery' (as Michael Arlen called it) of Whitehorse Street, and you find it just as it was when you saw it last. There are *cafés* (continental type with blue and white check table-cloths), cafés (English working class), old pubs, curio shops galore, a family grocer, a bakery baking its own bread, two or three restaurants, one called Shepherd's Pie and another named after Tiddy Dol, the gingerbread seller, with a notice outside which tells his story. There's a general air of *bonhomie*, everyone knows everyone else, and in the shops it's 'Hallo, Jack!' and 'Lovely day!' exchanged between friends over the counter.

Perhaps what makes it so different from the rest of Mayfair is the absence of traffic. There are no cars – at least they are all stationary as no one would think of driving through Shepherd Market. It is a little villagey bit of Mayfair that has survived, like Lancashire Court off New Bond Street, intimate and homely. No wonder tourists like to escape from Piccadilly and wander about its quaint streets, remarking 'It's like a little village', though, as we know, it was never a village in the real sense of the word; it was first a fair-ground, and then a market. The name Shepherd Market is carved in stone above the old three-storied market building in the centre, in case any one insists on calling it Shepherd's Market, but whatever its name or its origins this maze of narrow streets is the heart of Mayfair.

CHAPTER NINE

Hotels and Pubs

A FEW FRENCH CHEFS who had been in English service and a handful of ex-butlers can claim to be the first hotel keepers in Mayfair, the forerunners of the companies and financial groups which own Mayfair's many hotels today. The chefs and butlers with their experience of great country houses knew the requirements and tastes of the rich, and, with the aid of a capable wife, they ran highly successful establishments, two of them, Brown and Claridge, becoming household words, while the others have been forgotten with their hotels.

In Regency days Alexander Grillion, a Frenchman who had been chef in Lord Crewe's household for many years, was one of the earliest to set up a hotel. In 1803 he took a fine house in Albemarle Street, which was ceasing to be residential, and opened Grillion's Hotel there at No. 7, built by Sir John Norris in 1722, and now the headquarters of the National Book League.

The exiled King Louis XVIII stayed at Grillion's Hotel on his way through London to Paris to claim the throne of his ancestors, spending three nights under his compatriot's roof in Albemarle Street in April, 1814. Louis was enormously fat, and suffered from gout as well as dropsy, and he had the greatest difficulty in climbing the elliptical staircase, a feature of the Georgian house, which curves up in such a magnificent flight, 27 steps in all, from the hall. But he managed it with the aid of an arm lent by the Prince Regent, who was fat, too, and was led puffing and blowing into the drawing room on the first floor, hung with crimson velvet embroidered with the lilies of France in his honour, where His Most Christian Majesty received Lord Liverpool and his cabinet, the Diplomatic Corps and members of the old French nobility.

We are able to catch a glimpse of Alexander Grillion on this eventful day as Lady Crewe was present with Madame d'Arblay (Fanny Burney) who gives us an amusing portrait of Grillion being ordered about by his former mistress:

> We entered the hotel without difficulty, Lady Crewe having previously demanded a private room of Grillion, who had once been cook to her lord. This private room was at the back of the house, with a mere yard or common garden for its prospect. Lady Crewe declared this was quite too stupid, and rang the bell for waiter after waiter, till she made M. Grillion come himself. She then, in her singularly open and easy manner, told him to be so good as to order us a front room where we might watch for the arrival of the Royals, and be amused ourselves at the same time by seeing the entrance of the Mayor, Aldermen, and Common Councilmen, and other odd characters, who would be coming to pay their court to these French princes and princesses. M. Grillion gave a nod of acquiescence, and we were instantly shown to a front apartment just over the street door which was fortunately supplied with a balcony.

At the same time as Louis was staying at Grillion's another royal person, the Grand Duchess Catherine, sister of the Emperor of all the Russias, Alexander I, was lodging not far away at the Pulteney Hotel in Piccadilly where she watched the French king enter London in state from her balcony overlooking Green Park. The Pulteney Hotel was kept by a French chef too, Jean Escudier, and the Grand Duchess was accommodated there at the enormous cost of £210 a week which paid half the rate bill for a year, but hotels of this class could charge almost any price as there were so few of them. The Grand Duchess's stay in London started badly as she was still dressing when the Regent came to pay his respects and she was unable to receive him at the head of the stairs as she planned. They scowled at each other for the rest of the visit and she was not charmed either by the Regent's brother, the Duke of Clarence, who was considered as a possible husband for her. But the hotel vastly impressed her, and she wrote to her brother, the Emperor, who was due to arrive in England shortly, describing the Pulteney in glowing terms:

> April 1st, 1814.
> . . . *j'ai un hôtel garni, le plus beau de la ville . . . l'air de bien-être vous frapperait en tout et pour tout, ainsi que de certains arrangements de commodité dans les maisons, dont on n'a pas d'idée . . .*

The *certains arrangements de commodité* praised by the Grand Duchess in her quaint Russo-French referred without doubt to the Pulteney's water-closets. This early London hotel stood in the Piccadilly 'dip' at the corner of Brick Street opposite Lord Coventry's old house, and the Tyburn flowing under Brick Street would have served as a sewer for these pioneer water-closets. No. 105, Piccadilly corresponds roughly to the general outline of the old Pulteney Hotel, which was known as the Green Park Hotel, and later Hotel Splendide, between the wars.

The Emperor Alexander joined his sister at the Pulteney, much to the annoyance of the Regent who expected him to stay at bleak St James's Palace; and he appeared on the balcony of the hotel in reply to the cheers of crowds in Piccadilly.

Except for St James's Palace there was no royal residence where visiting royalty could stay. The old King was in the last stages of his madness at Windsor, Queen Charlotte was dying of dropsy at Kew, the Prince Regent would not put himself out for anyone at Carlton House, and the royal dukes were sunk in debt. When the hereditary Prince of Orange came to London to court Princess Charlotte, the Regent's daughter, he stayed with his tailor in Clifford Street. Even the future Queen of England, Princess Adelaide of Saxe-Meiningen, the bride-elect of the Duke of Clarence, experienced the inhospitality of the English Royal Family on her arrival from Germany with her mother in July, 1818. There was no royal reception for her when she landed at Deal and she had to wait three hours at Grillion's before the Regent came, unannounced, to pay her his respects, followed half an hour later by the Duke of Clarence himself, and she remained at the hotel until her marriage later in the month. (In parenthesis it might be stated that two years later Queen Caroline, the unfortunate wife of King George IV, had to make an unceremonious entry into London, too, staying, not at Grillion's Hotel, but nearby at 77, South Audley Street, as the guest of her friend, Alderman Wood, where she received formal addresses from the Common Council and Livery of London and appeared on the balcony and bowed to the crowd.)

A few years later we catch a glimpse of another royal visitor at Grillion's hotel, chronicled by Greville who wrote in a tone of shocked surprise that King William IV

> drove all over town in an open caleche with the Queen, Princess Augusta and the King of Wurtemberg, and coming home he set down

[Handwritten marginal notes:] 1760 – / Geo III 1820 / Geo P. of Wales / 1820–1830 / not Wm IV. / 1689–1702 / Wm IV / 1830–1837

the King (dropt him as he calls it) at Grillion's. The King of England dropping another King at a Tavern!

Greville let himself be carried away by his feelings, as Grillion's was nothing like a tavern, and was exceedingly well run and luxurious – like the Clarendon in New Bond Street, another early Mayfair hotel, kept by a Frenchman, too, Jacquier, who had been chef to Louis XVIII and subsequently to Lord Darnley. The Clarendon was famous for its French dinners which could cost, including a bottle of wine, as much as four guineas. But most visitors had to stay at taverns, and their discomfort was notorious as they had hardly changed since Shakespeare's time. The east of Piccadilly was lined with them, hostelries like the Black Bear, the White Bear, the Three Kings Inn (now Hatchett's is on the site), and other coaching inns whose hey-day ended with the coming of the railways. The most famous was the old Gloster Coffee House and Hotel which supplied 'good soups, dinners, wines and beds' in 1805. It was rebuilt as the St James's Hotel, later became the Berkeley Hotel under the directorship of Jules in 1897, and still has the inn's old stabling at the back in Dover Yard, alas to be demolished when the Berkeley Hotel moves to Knightsbridge.

The Clarendon, the largest hotel in London, had two entrances: at 160, New Bond Street on the site of Cartier's and at the back in Albemarle Street where carriages drew up owing to the lack of 'parking space' in the 'Bond Street Straits'. The front of the hotel in New Bond Street has vanished (Tallis reproduces it in his *Views*), but if we stand half way up Albemarle Street we can see the back of this early Mayfair hotel looking almost as it did in Regency days, when it was famous for its 'genuine French dinners'. To this day the old entrance to the Clarendon, No. 20, Albemarle Street, has an air of faded grandeur about it and cannot have greatly changed since the days when heavy family coaches and open barouches drove up from the country, and ostlers, grooms and hotel servants dashed out to attend to the wants of the new arrivals. The door is kept locked now, and it is nearly a hundred years since it admitted hotel guests as the Clarendon Hotel closed down in 1872, having ended its career under the management of Peter Grillion. He had moved over from No. 7, when his lease expired, bringing Grillion's Club, which had held meetings on the premises for over half a century, with him.

Albemarle Street used to be the centre of hotel life in London: more than half its fifty houses were hotels, kept mostly by ex-butlers with such names as Woodger's, Everatt's, Russell's, Gordon's (where Nelson stayed before Trafalgar), William's, Crawley's. . . .

There was another type of hotel in Mayfair, mostly frequented by an exclusive male clientele drawn from the sporting world. Stephen's and Long's, both in New Bond Street, almost opposite the Clarendon, belonged to this category, and they were run almost like clubs. Captain Gronow in his *Recollections and Anecdotes* tells us that if a stranger wanted to dine at Stephen's he was stared at by the servants and very solemnly assured that there was no table vacant. At the beginning of the century, according to Gronow, there was an élite of men of very high rank such as Wellington, Nelson, Collingwood and some sporting squires who never frequented the clubs, congregating at the fashionable hotels in the West End.

But because a hotel was exclusive it did not follow that the food was up to the standard of the French dinners which made the Clarendon so famous. Far from it. Limner's at the corner of George Street[1] and Conduit Street, also frequented by sporting types was 'the most dirty hotel in London', according to Gronow, who was of course exaggerating. But the English squirearchy were not distinguished by the delicacy of their manners, and were quite satisfied as long as there was plenty of good port and gin punch. Limner's was so crowded that a bed could not be had for love or money.

When the Duke of York sold York House in Piccadilly it was planned to convert it into the Royal York Hotel. Nothing came of the venture. Nevertheless, the Proprietors and Trustees of Albany agreed to find a desirable tenant to run a Dining Room and Hotel in the mansion facing Piccadilly. Several tenants tried their hand, but met with no success, and the hotel idea was abandoned. The premises were converted into chambers 'for the casual residence of the nobility and gentry who had no settled town residence' – and so Albany, the Regency community in Mayfair, was born.

The only hotel in this part of Mayfair to have survived is Brown's Hotel, started by James Brown, a butler who had been in Lord Byron's service. He began in a small way, as did all the others, with one house, then bought the houses next door, and finally sold out to J. J. Ford, who rebuilt the hotel as we know it today, Brown's Hotel in Dover Street, which was later amalgamated with the St George's Hotel in Albemarle Street. It was at Brown's that Theodore Roosevelt was staying when he drove off on a foggy December day in 1886 to be married to Edith

[1] Now St George Street.

159

Carow at St George's, wearing those bright orange gloves which Spring-Rice insisted upon. His portrait, presented by his daughter, Mrs Ethel Darby, in 1965, hangs in the Roosevelt Room – Franklin and Eleanor Roosevelt spent their honeymoon at Brown's in 1905.

The best known of the Albemarle Street hotels was the Hotel Albemarle, the high gabled, mottled pink building which still stands at the corner of Albemarle Street and Piccadilly facing down St James's Street. Originally Gordon's Hotel, where Byron and Nelson stayed, it became the Albe-marle Hotel in 1858. Whistler made a well-known etching of St James's Street, alive with hansoms, drawn from an upper window one June day in 1878. Sir Ernest George and Harold Peto rebuilt it in their 'François Premier' style in 1889 with – a surprising innovation – the kitchens at the top of the house. Given the more fashionable sounding name of the 'Hotel Albemarle' it became the smartest hotel in the West End in the 'nineties, patronised by 'royalty, the diplomatic corps and the nobility'. Oscar Wilde used to frequent it at the height of his fame. A room and attend-ance cost 7s., lunch 4s. and dinner 7s. to quote the prices in Baedeker's London of 1898, and non-residents wishing to lunch or dine in the Salle-à-Manger were requested 'to leave their names at the Bureau beforehand'.

It is surprising that the shell of the hotel – the interior is divided up into offices – has survived relatively untouched, yet few of the thousands, who crowd along Piccadilly, would guess of its association with the fashionable world of the fin-de-siècle. At No. 13, Albemarle Street, next to the Royal Arcade, was the Albemarle Club where the crazed Marquess of Queensberry left his offensive and ill-spelt card for Oscar Wilde, precipitating his ruin. The Pulteney Hotel had moved here from Pic-cadilly in 1823; and in the nineteen-twenties the Prince of Wales's favourite late night club, Uncle's, opened in the basement. Now Gieves, the naval and military outfitters and tailors, have their shop at No. 13, which has been rebuilt.

Next door at No. 14 is another ghost hotel, Carter's, where Lily Langtry used to stay. In those days the Blues were stationed at Albany Street Barracks, and they jingled through Mayfair, turning into Picca-dilly from Albemarle Street; just before reaching Carter's the signal was given and the band crashed out into a rollicking air which brought Lily Langtry waving and bowing to the window. Her balcony is still there, over a ladies' hairdressing salon.

The list of Mayfair's vanished hotels is a long one, but the public houses tell a different story. Perhaps because they are less exposed to

44. LONG'S HOTEL. Long's Hotel in New Bond Street at the corner of Clifford Street was a favourite haunt of sporting men in the last century. (Radio Times, Hulton Picture Library)

45. CLARIDGE'S HOTEL. Claridge's Hotel, formerly Mivart's, in Brook Street used to consist of several private houses run together.

46. HOTEL ALBEMARLE. The Hotel Albemarle, at the corner of Piccadilly and Albemarle Street, was was one of the smartest hotels in London in the 1890s. Oscar Wilde and Lord Alfred Douglas used to frequent it. It is now an office block. (Triplex Holdings Limited)

47. A FAMOUS NAME. The banker Nathan Rothschild gave a large party on July 4th, 1827, and one of the butlers provided by Gunter's, the famous Mayfair caterers, was John Claridge, whose son bought Mivart's Hotel in Brook Street. (Gunter and Company Ltd.)

changes of fashion and can be more easily brought up to date they seem to last longer than hotels. The pub-crawler can spend a whole evening in Mayfair revisiting the haunts of long ago.

On VE Day 1945 among all the congratulations which poured into 10, Downing Street was a telegram addressed to Mr Winston Churchill, as he then was, signed 'Duke of Albemarle'. The ducal telegram stood out from all the rest and caused quite a stir among the Prime Minister's staff. Debrett and other books of reference were consulted but no Duke of Albemarle could be found. The title was extinct. Was the telegram a hoax? Then one of the secretaries noticed the postal district where it had been handed in. It was London W1 and he put two and two together. It was from the public house called The Duke of Albemarle in Stafford Street.

The Duke of Albemarle is Mayfair's oldest pub, a quaint two storey house of dark red brick with white shutters at the corner of Dover Street and Stafford Street, which has stood here since Stafford Street was laid out on Albemarle Ground, and it is fitting that the old pub should be the guardian of Mayfair's celebrated relic, the Stafford Street sign, just inside the door on the right. The old pub has other links with the past – two pictures of Clarendon (later Albemarle) House, which hang in the Saloon Bar.

A few steps away is the Goat Tavern, of almost equal antiquity, though the house has been rebuilt. The ground is owned by the Vicar of St Martin's and the Rector of St George's, who are joint landlords, but in the legal sense of the word only. The Rector of St George's uses his portion of the rent for relieving the poor of the parish by providing them with clothes, boots and other necessities at Christmas.

The list of Mayfair's pubs is endless, and there are even three with the same name. 'The Coach and Horses': one in Hill Street, and the other two on the 'banks' of the Tyburn in Avery Row, and at the corner of Bruton Lane and Bruton Street. One pub has a very quaint name, unique in London, if not in the whole country, and certainly the longest: 'I am the only Running Footman' at the corner of Hays Mews and Charles Street patronised in olden days by the footmen, running and otherwise, of the great houses in Berkeley Square and the neighbourhood. It has moved with the times since then, and the saloon with its plush carpet and comfortable chairs is as smart as the cocktail bar of an expensive hotel. Its below-stairs customers are now on the walls in a series of coloured prints showing a stately house steward, a liveried coachman, a groom in dress and undress, a tiger and a page: and one huge picture of the running footman himself sprinting ahead of a coach in a cobbled street, a feather in his cap and carrying a wand, like the footman on the sign outside. A running footman's speed was about seven miles an hour and to maintain his strength he refreshed himself with sips of white wine and egg, a mixture he kept in the silver ball on the top of his wand.

The Duke of Queensberry – Old Q, a notorious Mayfair character who died in 1810 aged 86 – was the last nobleman to employ a running footman and he sent them after the ladies who caught his fancy as they passed by his house in Piccadilly. One footman was too clever for him. Being on approval, so to speak, he was dressed up in the Duke's gorgeous livery and told to show off his paces in Piccadilly. He ran well, and Old Q shouted from his balcony, 'You'll do for me'. 'And your livery will do very well for me,' shouted back the running footman and true to his name he ran out of sight.

Charles Street and Hill Street are unusual in Mayfair in so far as there is not a single shop in their entire length and they have changed very little outwardly. After the squares these two streets and Curzon Street were the epitome of fashionable Mayfair, and Ralph Nevill writing in 1928 in *Romantic London* can remember Charles Street in the eighteen-seventies and 'eighties when it was

> full of carriages and fine horses during the season and a dignified butler and two footmen stood ready at almost every door to receive visitors coming to pay calls.

The multitude of men servants in Mayfair – two or three to each house – help to explain the number of public houses, as they were certainly not patronised by the aristocratic residents except furtively. Mayfair had two layers of population in those days: the residents whose names were in the Red Books and Green Books of London society living in the patrician houses which are now shops, clubs, antique showrooms, couturier salons, ladies' hairdressers, offices, workrooms and gaming clubs; and the humbler world of butlers, footmen, coachmen, grooms, pages, gardeners, stable hands and countless female servants of varying degree. The houses were appallingly difficult to run; bathrooms were unknown, and every drop of water and lump of coal had to be carried up the narrow back stairs.

Charles Street becomes a lane at the far end leading uphill to the Red Lion, one of Mayfair's most secluded and attractive pubs, with low

ceilinged rooms and cosy nooks which cannot have greatly changed
since it clung like a limpet to the wall of Chesterfield House garden and
was a favourite resort of the below-stairs population of that great house.
One more old-fashioned Mayfair pub, the Punch Bowl, is quite close,
at the end of South Street where it joins Farm Street. It has, also, merci-
fully escaped being turned into a cocktail bar, and looks as it did in
Georgian days when its saloon and public bar (divided by a wooden
partition) were filled with coachmen and grooms from nearby Berkeley
Mews. Today Mayfair's businessmen crowd in at midday when four are
needed to serve behind the bar, but at night time when the streets are
quiet and the kitchen clock in the saloon ticks away towards eleven
o'clock business quietens down, and the door only opens now and again
to admit a chauffeur who has finished for the evening, or a footman from
a catering firm, who has just served dinner in a small mews house or flat,
wearing his livery under his mackintosh.

A narrow alleyway between the houses in South Street leads into the
peace of St George's Hanover Square Garden, the old graveyard, and
passing the seats with their inscriptions and the Lofts-George drinking
fountain we are back among the red houses of Mount Street, and almost
facing the graceful curve of the Connaught Hotel in Carlos Place built
of red brick to harmonise with Sir Ernest George's street.

A much older hotel stood here when Carlos Place was called Charles
Street: Wauthier's Coburg Hotel named in honour of the Prince Consort's family. It was later taken over by one of the Grillion dynasty,
and rebuilt from the ground up in the characteristic Palm Court Hotel
style of the eighteen-nineties by Sir Blundell Maple. A nostalgic Palm
Court atmosphere lingers there still. There is no chromium or glass,
no name in neon lights; the public rooms have high ceilings and the
lounge is like a spacious sitting room in a country house, with the
mahogany bookcase filled with old volumes of *Punch*.

The hotel anglicised its name from Coburg to Connaught in the first
World War owing to the public outcry at the unrestricted U-boat
warfare; the Duke of Connaught gave his permission for it to be called
after him. It is a relatively small hotel of 100 rooms only, and the guests
enjoy great privacy and comfort. It is the favourite hotel of Prince
Rainier and Princess Grace of Monaco.

The royal hostelry *par excellence* is Claridge's in Brook Street which
was opened in November, 1898, the year after the Connaught; Lady de
Grey, the leader of London society, laid its foundation stone. The

choice of such an important social figure to perform the ceremony was a pointer to the new rôle of the hotel in Mayfair, a rôle which has continued to increase ever since.

Claridge's history is similar to the Connaught's, as it also began in a small way, and was originally kept by a French chef, Jacques Mivart, who started business in two houses in Brook Street, on the present site, in the year of Waterloo when so many important visitors crowded into London. Mivart like his compatriots, Grillion, Escudier and Jacquier, prospered exceedingly, fulfilling the needs of English county families who, half frozen in their draughty homes and suffering from a surfeit of joints, fowls, puddings and port, appreciated the variety and subtlety of French cooking. The Prince Regent had a suite of rooms reserved for him here.

Mivart's soon established the reputation of being 'the usual residence of sovereign princes and other foreigners of distinction', and we find Mrs Gore, that indefatigable chronicler of the fashionable world, writing in her novel, *The Diamond and the Pearl*, that

> Lord and Lady Downham were perceived at Emms and Kissingen to be surrounded by Highnesses royal and serene and Russian princes sufficient to have peopled Mivart's Hotel.

Mivart's – or is it Grillion's or the Pulteney? – is 'the sweetest of hotels' in Byron's *Don Juan*, Canto XI:

> They reach'd the hotel; forth stream'd from the front door
> A tide of well-clad waiters, and around
> The mob stood, and as usual several score
> Of those pedestrian Paphians who abound
> In decent London when the daylight's o'er;
> Commodious but immoral, they are found
> Useful, like Malthus, in promoting marriage –
> But Juan now is stepping from his carriage.
> Into one of the sweetest of hotels,
> Especially for foreigners – and mostly
> For those whom favour or whom fortune swells. . . .

Mivart continued to preside over his distinguished hotel for nearly forty years when he was succeeded by the first Englishman to make an international reputation as a hotelier, William Claridge, the son of that John Claridge who was hired out from Gunter's for Nathan Rothschild's great party in 1827. He had already been running a small hotel in Brook Street next to Mivart's and amalgamated the two, but wisely kept on the famous name 'Mivart's Hotel' for some years and only gradually replaced it by his own, adding 'late Mivart's' underneath. Queen Victoria gave Claridge's her seal of approval when with the Prince Consort she called there to visit Empress Eugénie who was staying at the royal hostelry during her visit to London in 1860.

This was the time when many new hotels were being built in London like the luxurious Langham Hotel in Portland Place, a colossus with 700 rooms, a winter garden, 'ascending rooms' as lifts were called then, and even a post office, compared with which Claridge's was downright stuffy and old-fashioned. Countess Marie Larisch, the niece of the Empress Elizabeth of Austria, found it 'a dark uncomfortable place' in 1877 when she was staying there with her aunt and a swarm of foreign royalties.

Nevertheless Baedeker's *London* in its first edition of the following year lists Claridge's as 'the first hotel in London', and one cannot help feeling that a hotel was judged not so much by its size, position, modern conveniences or even cuisine as by the status of its guests. Royalty and other splendid people would never have dreamed of staying at such 'a vulgar place' as the Langham or the new Grand Hotel in Northumberland Avenue. They remained faithful to Mr Claridge, and his hotel was mentioned in the same breath as the Hotel Bristol in Paris and the Beau Rivage at Ouchy overlooking the Lake of Geneva, though Claridge's consisted of only half a dozen houses knocked into one and had no view except of a row of similar houses opposite; but its guests breathed the same air as the residents of both Grosvenor Square and Berkeley Square which were just round the corner.

William Claridge sold his hotel to a company for £60,000 in 1881, a hundred years after the birth of his predecessor Mivart, and the following year he died at his home, Cragthorne, Grove Park, Kent. For a few years the old-fashioned hotel, and it was really behind the times now, continued to attract its traditional clientele of crowned heads, but finally change had to come and in 1895 the Savoy Group bought it and pulled down the famous row of old houses. The furniture and effects were put up to auction and one of the lots, a large gilt mirror from the royal suite shaded in black in mourning for Queen Adelaide, was knocked down to a young sporting bachelor who had chambers in Albany, Mr William Stone. It now graces the Secretary's chambers there, occupying a place of honour over the marble chimney-piece, reflecting the ghosts of emperors and empresses, kings and queens, and 'highnesses royal and serene' who used to stay at Claridge's, 'late Mivart's'.

The new Claridge's built by Sir Ernest George, the architect of so much *fin de siècle* red brick Mayfair, rising to nine storeys with lifts and electric light and bathrooms, was so revolutionary that the new management thought it advisable to warn the hotel's regular patrons that

> the spirit of modernism in the nine storey building would not in the least interfere with their comfort and privacy.

The royal suite on the first floor had a separate entrance from Davies Street. The suite is still there but the entrance has been replaced, and so has the old *porte cochère* in Brook Street intended for hansoms and carriages which could turn inside the small court yard, but it was not built for the motor age.

In the Edwardian era no blatant dance bands as yet disturbed the aristocratic quiet of Mayfair, and the two new *hotels de luxe* still conformed to the old principle that a hotel should be first and foremost a home from home for its guests. However, non-residents were beginning to frequent Claridge's, and in the last seasons before the first World War it was becoming fashionable to have lunch in the restaurant or take tea in the drawing room among the palms, served by the liveried footmen, who still wait on Claridge's guests today.

With the end of the war, Mayfair's new hotel era started in earnest. A memory of those years is of the two rusting cage-like structures in the Piccadilly 'dip' where the construction of Mayfair's latest hotel, the Park Lane, had been halted by the war and was not resumed until some years later. The new hotel occupied one of the finest sites in Mayfair overlooking Green Park not far away from the old Pulteney Hotel, which was a century before its time: it was now the site that mattered, and the days when Mayfair's smart hotels could be hidden away in quiet streets belonged to the past. Fine sites were going begging, and the builders of the new hotels could take their choice as one grand mansion after another was demolished.

With the destruction of Devonshire House the old clause about not building on the south side of Berkeley Square lapsed and in 1927 the May Fair Hotel, reviving an old name, was built at the lower end of Devonshire House garden, commanding a fine view of the square until the new red brick block of Lansdowne House flats rose up on the adjoining garden of Lansdowne House.

On Mayfair's western frontier startling changes overtook Park Lane, for here were the best sites of all for the new hotels, commanding sweeping views of Hyde Park. In the late 1920s London's two celebrated hotels, Grosvenor House and the Dorchester, soared over the trees and by the time the war broke out both had established themselves as London institutions, while the houses which stood on the island sites originally – the mansion of the Duke of Westminster and the Italian *palazzo* with its magnificent staircase built to last a millenium by Vulliamy in 1852 – are now almost forgotten.

Very few bombs fell on Mayfair. One of the isolated casualties was the Victorian mansion 145, Piccadilly, King George VI's house when he was Duke of York. Yet Mayfair was a legitimate target, as Grosvenor Square, where General Eisenhower had his headquarters, was the nerve centre of the American war effort.

For ten years after the war there were few changes in Mayfair while this fashionable part of London took stock of itself. But by the mid-fifties the pre-war juggernaut started moving again, directed at the last pockets of residents holding out in private houses and flats to the west of the old Tyburn boundary between Bond Street and Park Lane. Many of the old Georgian houses which were bulldozed had ceased to be residential, but their loss is nevertheless deplorable. However, in the rebuilding of Mayfair, there have been several encouraging signs. The new hotels built since the war, the Westbury, Hilton, Europa and now Londonderry House, show that Mayfair is still the most desirable part of London in which to stay. But visitors to London do not want to be surrounded by office blocks, and it is encouraging that nearly 250 years after Sir Richard Grosvenor planned his estate his square is still mainly residential thanks to the enlightened policy of the Grosvenor Estate in rebuilding it as a unit. Nevertheless, if its two remaining Georgian houses are pulled down the loss will be lamentable. Many blocks of flats have been built, and Mayfair enters its fourth century since Lord Clarendon built the first house on these fields as still residential in part. Any plan to put up more blocks for day time staff only should be stoutly resisted.

Now it is time to mount the 328 feet high tower of the London Hilton in Park Lane to look down from the 28th floor on the streets and squares, the churches and houses which have been the subject of this book.

When Lord Clarendon built his house, rolling fields filled in the view below us, and at the foot of the tower was Brookfield, where the May Fair was held. We can still look right into Shepherd Market and see

Sunderland House standing on the site of the Mayfair Chapel where Dr Keith carried on his notorious marriage business. Beyond Shepherd Market the grey mass of Devonshire House emerges at the point in Piccadilly where the turnpike used to stand marking the western limit of London in Queen Anne's reign. The three large blocks to the left of it stretching one behind the other to the trees of Berkeley Square show the line of old Devonshire House garden and the garden of Lansdowne House adjoining it, once a belt of green in the heart of the West End.

Grosvenor Square, less thickly planted with trees than Berkeley Square, looks impressive from this height, and the new pink and white blocks on the northern side are distinctive. We can see the two remaining Georgian houses of Grosvenor Square, Nos. 43 and 44, from the back, and, if the leaves are off the trees, look into the paved garden of No. 44 and see the french window of the old dining room where the Waterloo Despatch was brought by Henry Percy.

Of Mayfair's churches and chapels, St George's steeple is difficult to pick out against the background of grey roofs. But the sky-blue spire of the Grosvenor Chapel points upward as it should, and we have a clear view of the gothic front of the Church of the Immaculate Conception in Farm Street, built originally in imitation of the west front of Beauvais Cathedral, but renovated after being bombed. Another church which stands up well is the Christian Science temple in Curzon Street, beyond Shepherd Market.

The street cutting in a straight line through the houses northward from the foot of the Hilton is South Audley Street with its continuation North Audley Street, an impressive thoroughfare seen from this height, prolonged beyond Mayfair's northern frontier by Baker Street to Regent's Park.

One can see or trace all four of Mayfair's frontiers: the full northward sweep of Park Lane to Marble Arch, the tall buildings marking the northern boundary of Oxford Street with Marylebone beyond, the curve of Regent Street's high roofs, and Piccadilly where it flows past Devonshire House and reappears through the gap in old Park Lane, once such a notorious bottle-neck, to join the whirligig of traffic at Hyde Park Corner – the frontiers which, as Sydney Smith said, 'enclosed more intelligence, human ability, to say nothing of wealth and beauty than the world ever collected in so small a space before'.

The frontiers are standing firm in spite of changes, and Mayfair still remains a town within a town.

Books Consulted

Anon. *Wonderful London. Its Lights and Shadows, Humour and Sadness* (1878)
Anon. (James Ralph). *A New Critical Review of the Publick Buildings, Statues and Ornaments in and about London and Westminster* (1736)
S. N. Behrman. *Duveen*
Sheila Birkenhead. *Peace in Piccadilly*
E. Beresford Chancellor. *The History of the Squares of London*
E. Beresford Chancellor. *The Private Palaces of London*
G. Clinch. *Mayfair and Belgravia*
A. I. Dasent. *A History of Grosvenor Square*
A. I. Dasent. *Piccadilly*
Bernard Folk. *The Berkeleys of Berkeley Square*
Roger Fulford. *The Royal Dukes*
C. T. Gatty. *Mary Davies and the Manor of Ebury*
Ivor Halstead. *Bond Street*
E. Hatton. *A New View of London* (1708)
H. Montgomery Hyde. *Londonderry House*
B. H. Johnson. *Berkeley Square to Bond Street*
W. J. Loftie. *A History of London*
Grand-Duc Nicolas Mikailowitch. *Correspondance de l'Empereur Alexandre 1er avec sa soeur*
The National Book League. *7, Albemarle Street*
Ralph Nevill. *Mayfair and Montmartre*
Ralph Nevill. *Romantic London*
Ralph Nevill and Charles Edward Jerningham. *Piccadilly to Pall Mall*
George Paston. *At John Murray's, 1843–1892*
Thomas Pennant. *Account of London* (1791)
Professor N. Pevsner. *Cities of London and Westminster*
Frederick A. Pottle (Editor). *Boswell's London Journal*
Giles St Aubyn. *The Royal George*
G. Smith and F. Benger. *The Oldest London Bookshop, 1728–1928*

John Summerson. *Georgian London*
Survey of London. Vol. xxxii. *Parish of St James's North of Piccadilly*
H. B. Wheatley. *A Short History of Bond Street*
H. B. Wheatley. *London Past and Present*
Geoffrey Williamson. *Star-Spangled Square*

Index

INDEX

Chemistry, Royal College of, Hanover Square, 59

Chesham, John Compton, 4th Baron, 139

Chesterfield, Philip Stanhope, 4th Earl of, 71, 76, 93, 117–118

Chesterfield, Philip Stanhope, 5th Earl of, 68

Chesterfield Gardens, formerly John Street, 74

Chesterfield House, South Audley Street, 97–98
  Dr Johnson at, 118
  Princess Mary's home, 93
  flats, 103

Chez Victor, nightclub, 95

Childe Harold, 119

Christ Church, Down Street, 78

Christ Scientist, Third Church of, Curzon Street, 79

Church Commissioners: *see* Ecclesiastical Commissioners

Church Parade in Hyde Park, 78

Churchill, Lord Randolph, death at 50, Grosvenor Square, 57

Churchill, Sir Winston, 57

Clarence, Albert Victor, Duke of, memorial window, 75

Clarendon, Edward Hyde, Earl of, 28, 29, 30, 36

Clarendon Hotel, New Bond Street, 125, 158

Clarendon House, later Albemarle House, 28–29, 112, 161

Clarges, Thomas, 33

Claridge, John, butler at Nathan Rothschild's party, 141

Claridge, William, 164–165

Claridge's Hotel, Brook Street, 125, 163–166

Clark, Wyndham, 41

Clermont Club, Berkeley Square, 41

Clifford Street, Dickens's tailor, 125
  Prince of Orange stays with his tailor, 157

Clive, Robert, 1st Baron (Clive of India), 41

Coach and Horses, public house, Bruton Street, 17
  Avery Row, 161
  Hill Street 161

Coburg Hotel: *see* Connaught Hotel

Cockerell, C. R., architect, 80

Collignon, Charles, physician, 117

Colman, George, playwright, 134

Comper, Sir Ninian, architect, 76

Conduit Street, 34, 69

Coningsby, 121

Connaught, Arthur, Duke of, 43, 163

Connaught Hotel, Carlos Place, 163

Cooper, Sir Astley, physician, 34

Cork Street, 34, 35

Corrigan, Mrs James, 107

Corsair, The, 119

Courtauld, Samuel, 109

Courtauld, Major Stephen, 57

Coutts, Thomas, banker, 123

Coventry, George, 6th Earl of, house in Grosvenor Square, 58
  complains of Fair, 26

Crauford, John, 116

Crawley's Hotel, Albemarle Street, 159

Crewe, Henrietta, Lady, 156

Crewe, John, 2nd Baron, 155

Crewe, Robert, Marquess of, 92, 98–99

Crewe House (Wharncliffe House), 69, 98–99

Croker, John Wilson, politician and essayist, 119

Croly, the Rev. George, author of *May Fair*, 123n

Cross, John Walter: *see* George Eliot

Culross Street, Park Lane, 106

Cumberland, Henry Frederick, Duke of (1745–1790), morganatic marriage to Mrs Horton, 83

Cunard, Maud (Emerald), Lady, 58

Cundy, Thomas, architect, 104

Curiosities of Natural History, 58

Curzon, Sir Nathaniel, 22

Curzon Chapel: *see* Mayfair Chapel

Curzon Place (formerly Seamore Place), 103, 153n

Curzon Street, 103
  Disraeli's house, 122
  Becky Sharp's house, 126–127
  Mrs Erlynne, 128

Dahl Michael, artist, 58

Daily Advertiser, 71

Daily Journal, 47

Daily Telegraph, The, 91

d'Arblay, Madame (Fanny Burney), 156

Darby, Mrs Ethel: *see* Brown's Hotel

Dartmouth House, English-Speaking Union, Charles Street, 42

Dasent, Arthur, London historian, 58

Davies, Alexander, father of Mary Davies, buried in St Margaret's, 46

Davies, Rev. C. M., author, 75

Davies, Mary (Lady Grosvenor), 45–47

Davies Street, 47

Delane, John, Editor of *The Times*, 101

Devonshire, Georgiana, Duchess of, 37
  theft of Gainsborough portrait of, 143–144

Devonshire, Louise, Duchess of ('The Double Duchess'), 28, 37, 55
  married 8th Duke of Devonshire, 79

Devonshire, Spencer-Compton, 8th Duke of, 27

Devonshire, Victor, 9th Duke of, 43

Devonshire, William, 1st Duke of, 32, 33, 43

Devonshire, William, 4th Duke of, 36

Devonshire, William, 6th Duke of, 36–37

Devonshire House, formerly Berkeley House, 27–28, 30–33, 36–38, 43, 112, 125, 126, 130

Diamond and the Pearl, The, 164

Dick, Sir William Reid, 56

Dickens, Charles, 125–126

Disraeli, Benjamin (Earl of Beaconsfield), buys suits in Cork Street, 35
  marriage at St George's, 64
  at Grosvenor Gate, 106, 120
  death in Curzon Street, 122

Disraeli, Mrs (Mrs Wyndham Lewis), 64, 106

d'Israeli, Isaac, author, 119

Dodd, Dr William, divine, hanged for forgery at Tyburn, 68–69

Dog-stealing, 146

Dolly Sisters, 44

INDEX

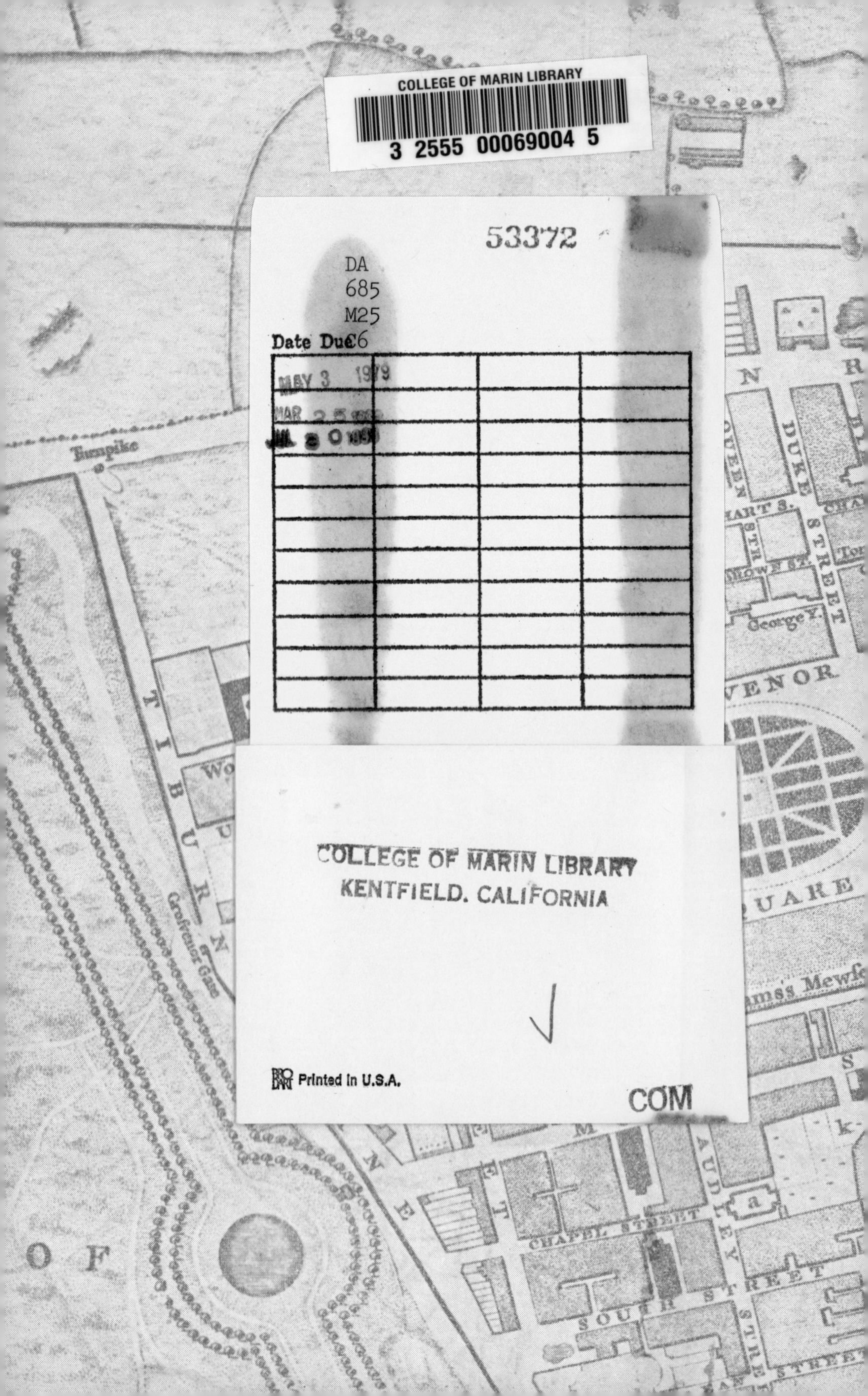
Turnpike
TIBURN
Grosvenor Gate
QUEEN
DUKE STREET
George Y.
VENOR
UARE
SOUTH STREET
CHAPEL STREET
AUDLEY
O F